MY
Village
SPEAKS

Parenting, Mentoring, Educating, and Sharing

love

acceptance peace

loss pain

forgiveness

By MARY HALLIDAY

Thank you for your support.

I tried to capture the strength
of the black family despite
our trials and tribulations.
Let me know if I succeeded.
Call me 215 476 9858

Mary Halliday
Nov. 17, 2016

FOREWORD

Mary Halliday is a 74-year-old matriarch in her family. She is a retired social worker. She speaks about faith and family. Her story begins with the trials and tribulations of her grandparents and her parents. The migration of her relatives from the South to the North in the 1930s, their entrepreneurial spirit, and the impact WWII had on her family.

Mary includes the excitement of marriage and motherhood and the brokenness of separation, divorce, and being a single parent.

The matriarch and historian of the family, she explores the impact of economic, social, and legislative systems, as well as religious beliefs, customs, and practices on families and neighborhoods in a village.

She has traveled to many countries trying to develop a greater insight into the human spirit. The mindset of the "Ruling Class," whether they are black or white, in the USA, Africa, Caribbean, or other countries.

She looks at the customs of parenting, mentoring, educating, and passing down the history and legacy of people in many countries around the world.

She realizes that it is important for every nationality to know and understand African history because we are the seat of civilization. However, we need to know and understand the history and legacy of other nationalities also.

Everything is relevant because we are all related as human beings.

"Each one, teach one." -Frank Laubach

ACKNOWLEDGEMENTS

Hakimah Reese typed and edited this entire book.
The following family and friends helped edit this book:
Geraldine Foster, Tanya Alexander, Connie McClenney, Delores Jackson, Zenobia Boulware, Damon Halliday, Julianne James, Kenya Halliday, Kendra Halliday, Father Paul Wise, Dr. Steven Jones, Trudy Mitchell, Bakari Jackson, and Deidre King. My great-granddaughters Kayliana and Kapri Halliday also gave insightful input that I used during the editing of this book.

Posthumously:

I want to thank my cousins, Blanch and Herman Nixon, as well as James and Viola Drummond for their love, encouragement, and faith. Especially while attending the University of Pennsylvania Graduate School of Social Work full-time and working full-time. I was also taking care of my sick mother and sending two children to college.

Viola and Blanch were both sick and I could not visit or help them like I wanted to. They kept telling me not to worry about them, and to stay focused because they knew that I could do it.

I also thank Eunice Walden, Earline and Pearline Parks, and Massey Telford. My parents worked nights, and sometimes weekends, and they were always there to babysit, encourage, and love me throughout my childhood.

TABLE OF CONTENTS

I.   Acknowledgements vii

II. Inspiration xv

III. Motivation xvii

IV. Introduction xix

V.   Dedicated to: Victims and Children of Rape xxiii

VI. Pictures of My Village as A Child xxix

Chapter 1—Life in My Village 43

The Village Is Formed 43

Children Remember Joy 43

Children Remember Trauma 44

Angry with God 44

Family Historian 44

My Oldest Brother 45

Talking to a Dying Christian 45

    His Eulogy 46

Chapter 2—The Extended Family Within the Village 47

Significance of First Cousins 47

Chapter 3—Neighbors in The Village 48

Chapter 4—Ghetto! What Ghetto? 49

The GI Bill 49

Subsidized Housing 50

Funerals at home 50

Chapter 5—Guns, Gangs and Mothers 51

Homeless but Hopeful..........................52

Chapter 6—Entrepreneurs 54

Chapter 7—The War Boost the Economy..........................55

Minimum Wage..........................56

Paycheck to paycheck 56

Industrial Revolution: Opportunity 57

Good Old Times: Respect 57

Chapter 8—The Culture of Poverty/The Culture of Congress 60

Drug Dealing..........................62

Slavery Today 62

Unions vs. Insituitional Racism 62

Chapter 9—Hope 64

U.S. Office for Educational Rights 64

STEM (Science, Technology, Engineering and Math)..........................64

Women in The Trades In New York 65

Opportunities Industrialization Center 65

2 Current Organizations: We're Still Rising 65

Chapter 10—What Happened to Black Entrepreneurs? 66

Chapter 11—Family and Friends Will Help You 68

Trouble in The Air 68

Remember This 70

Chapter 12—I Got a New Dad 72

Chapter 13—Body Language 74

Chapter 14—Ritalin: Kiddie Crack 76

Where is daddy? 77

Chapter 15—Institutional Racism 80

Chapter 16—Labels: Against All Odds 82

Chapter 17—School Dropout 84

Suicidal 85

Girls Need Their Father's Too 85

Chapter 18—Chronological Age vs. Developmental Age 87

Chapter 19—Independence 89

Look for The Good 89

Damon's Teachers Spoke Highly of Him 89

Our Neighbors Spoke Highly of Him 90

My Pastor Predicted He Would Preach 90

Marijuana 90

Pray Without Ceasing 91

Chapter 20—Letter from Mother To Son 92

Chapter 21—I Couldn't Pray 93

Chapter 22–Sick: But Not unto Death 94

Transferred Grief..95

Angel in Disguise...95

Sick Again: But Covered by The Blood 96

Chapter 23—Developing A Reprobate Mind.............................97

Chapter 24—Shame 99

Stop! Turn Your Mess into A Message......................................99

Chapter 25—Sin..101

Chapter 26—God says: Avoid Too Much Food and Wine 102

God says: Avoid Adultery 102

God says: Avoid Gangs 103

Chapter 27—Be Somebody in Christ 104

Chapter 28—Our Foreparents: Our Forerunners 105

Chapter 29–Church 106

Six Generations Later 106

Do Not Sit in The Counsel Of The Ungodly 106

Deacons of The Church..106

Deaconess of The Church 107

Wind Beneath My Wings 108

Chapter 30—Visionaries 109

Chapter 31—Marriage: God's Family Plan 111

Couples Working Together 112

Being of One Mind and One Spirit 112

Being Evenly Yoked 112

Chapter 32—Amazing Men 114

Chapter 33–Welfare, School and Work 118

Phenomenal Women 118

Chapter 34—Broken Marriage Not Broken Children 120

Chapter 35—Join A Coalition: Don't Isolate Yourself 122

Strongholds in The Village 122

Chapter 36- Lows and Highs of Retirement 124

Lowest Points 124

Highest Points 124

Free to Travel 124

Chapter 37–Travel Broadens Your Perspective 125

Understanding The Human Spirit 125

Egypt: Art Before Christ 125

Coptic Christians Persecuted 125

Ghana: Liberating Ghana 126

South Africa: Apartheid Ends 127

Coming to America 129

Middle class lifestyle: the same 129

Trinidad: Suicide Among Teenagers 129

Chapter 38—Don't Tell Your Children 131

Chapter 39—Holocaust Survivors 133

Chapter 40—Experiencing One of the Wonders of The World 134

Chapter 41—Recalibrate Your Life 135

Chapter 42—Healing The Village..137

INSPIRED BY:

I am inspired by my two children, Damon and Kenya Halliday. I am proud of the way they have grown and matured. They have faced the many changes living has brought into their lives and adapted. I can see their spiritual and personal growth.

I have learned that while we try to teach our children all about life, our children teach us what life is all about.

MOTIVATED BY:

There have been many shows on television that reflect the times and experiences in my life. I recently felt motivated to tell my story and reflect on the relativity of these shows and how they evoked certain memories and feelings in my life.

Oprah Winfrey's show *Oprah: Where Are They Now?* featuring military heroes returning home from Iraq brings back memories of the men in my family returning home from World War II. I was only four years old, but I remember each homecoming and how I felt as if it were yesterday. I also remember the day the war ended.

I have heard many people say that *The Cosby Show* was not real or relevant to black families, but it was real in the village that I grew up in. My house and my neighborhood looked similar to theirs. My parents had the same dreams and values that the Cosby's portrayed in the Huxtable family. My parents put the best interest and well being of their children first, regardless of what was going on in their marriage, the community, or the world.

Tyler Perry's character Madea reminds me of my Aunt Essie. She was tall, strong, hilarious, full of life, and threatening. She never hurt anyone, but everyone was afraid to test her.

On Oprah Winfrey's Sunday night show *Life Class*, Oprah and Iyana's discussion about sons and daughters without fathers and living paycheck to paycheck was real to me as a single parent.

My parents and most of my relatives owned businesses between the 1930s and 1970s. I can relate to the issues and the sacrifices of the families on Oprah Winfrey's show *Sweetie Pie*.

The movie *Outsourcing* reminds me of when industrialists moved jobs to foreign countries. It changed the livelihood of families who would have been considered middle class in the village.

There have been many Christian programs on television that emphasize the scripture that my mother taught me. "Those who are held in the highest esteem among men are held in abomination in the sight of God" (Luke 16: 15). They stink in his nostrils and they will answer to him.

"Then I will tell them plainly, 'I never knew you. Away from me, you evil-doers!'" (Matt. 7:23).

In my mother's words, "What would you give in exchange for your soul?"

INTRODUCTION:

IT TAKES A VILLAGE TO RAISE A CHILD

I have stayed connected to my village. They know my story and they have provided me with wise counsel. All of the resources that I need are in the village. I had to keep an open mind and an open heart to identify them and to utilize them at the appropriate time to meet specific needs.

Now that I am a senior citizen with three generations following me, the puzzle is beginning to come together. I have to include my life and circumstances before birth until the present time to see the impact.

Yes, my family including my grandparents and I have been broken at times by different circumstances, but we can also see how we are blessed and highly favored.

In my younger years, I thought that I was just living day to day feeding on and responding to whatever my circumstances were at that time. But now I can see where each stage of my life was preparation for the next stage or set of circumstances that I would face.

I heard someone say that, "My setback was my setup for my comeback." Well, I can see that clearly in my life now.

Early childhood development theories state that, "A child's most formative years take place between birth and five years old." I learned in my early years of development how it felt to be loved, as well as, how people should live and treat each other, along with the importance of organization and structure.

I also had the experience of responding to tragedy and loss, and how it affected my family and me. It is disruptive and it's hard to get your footing and balance back. You have to regroup and recalculate every aspect of your life, mostly financial, but keeping as much organization and tradition in place during this time of transition is helpful.

The picture on the front cover is my ex-husband and my son during the times when I thought I had a good and healthy marriage. What happened? What went wrong? Why didn't I see it coming? Well, I still can't tell you that I have all the answers to those questions. But I did learn a great deal from the experiences of being a single parent, and I know that I gained the strength in my childhood for the storms that would come into my life as an adult.

I learned that I could not be everything to my children, even when I was with my husband. My children were my first love and responsibility. However, I had to leave room for each member of the family to continue to grow and adapt to change as we matured, including myself. I could not take away all of their pain or fix them. There are some tragedies in life that we have to accept and process on our own, regardless of age.

There are too many outside influences impacting our children's lives. Home and family are the first and most important, but in some cases we can see that they weren't even the greatest.

If you can eventually accept and adjust to your loss by death, sickness, or separation, the children will too. It's not easy on anyone in the family, but living with the new pleasures and challenges of each day will keep you busy and ease your grief. Don't keep holding them and apologizing to your children, you're passing your guilt and anxiety onto them. Talk to your friends, they know half of your story anyway and they have your ear.

"We can tell our children that loss is hard, but morning by morning new mercies we'll see, for great is thy faithfulness" (Lam. 3:23).

By writing this book I am celebrating my life while I can still see, taste, smell, hear and feel my life as a whole and the people that I love. In other words, I want to explore the world that shaped my life.

My favorite song is "When I look back over my life and I think things over, I can truly say that I've been blessed."

SCRIPTURE THAT I LIVE BY:

Yes, there is poverty, dysfunction and crime in the village, but everything you need is there too. Continue to look for and struggle towards:

"Whatever is true, whatever is noble, whatever is right, whatever is pure, whatever is lovely, whatever is admirable-if anything is excellent or praiseworthy-focus on those things and put them into practice, and the God of peace will be with you" (Phil. 4:8–9).

All scripture quoted in this book is from the New International Version (NIV) of The Bible.

DEDICATED TO: VICTIMS AND CHILDREN OF RAPE

I dedicate this book to my maternal grandmother Lillian Pitts, who was a victim of rape, and to other mothers who were rape victims.

This book is also dedicated to my mother, Lenora Pitts, who was a child conceived by rape.

My mother Lenora says she met my father George Drummond when she was fifteen years old. She was homeless and living with different relatives. Her mother was sick with thyroid cancer. Her younger sister, Essie, was nine years old and her little brother, Lannie, was five years old. They were also living with different relatives.

Their father Jiles Pitts left them because he had a fight with a white man and the Ku Klux Klan was going to hang him. He said he was going up North to find a job and he would come back for them. They never heard from him again so they assumed they caught and hanged him.

So, Mommy met Daddy and they got married. My Dad and his brothers built a house for Mommy and her family. Then grandmother Lillian, Aunt Essie, and Uncle Lannie all moved into their new home.

One year later, when my grandmother Lillian was dying, she told my mother her true story. She was a rape victim. Her mother told her that she was engaged to Jiles Pitts when she was nineteen years old. Jiles had a cousin named Jimmy who was married to Lillian's best friend, Ann. Ann was very sick and she could not take care of her children. Jimmy and Jiles came together and asked her to babysit Jimmy and Ann's children because Jimmy had to work at night.

The first morning when he came home from work, he raped my grandmother.

She didn't tell anyone; she just did not go back. When she realized that she was pregnant, she told her fiancé. They went to Jimmy and Ann together and told them. Jiles told Jimmy that he was going to marry her anyway and take care of the baby, but they never wanted anything to do with them ever again. Jiles married Lillian before my mother was born and gave her his last name, Pitts.

My mother says her father, Jimmy, and his family lived in the neighborhood and she knew him and his wife and children, but they were never neighborly. My grandmother told my mother that if she ever needed anything after she died, she could go to him and his wife and they would help her.

My Mommy says they came to her mother's funeral and he and his wife came to her and told her the same thing. That was the first and last time they ever spoke to each other. Mommy says that her mother didn't turn to him when she was sick and homeless, so she vowed that she would not either, but she had my dad.

Her mother told her that she was dying and leaving her at sixteen with a ten-year-old sister and a six-year-old brother, and nobody knew what was going to happen in the future. She told my mother not to be too prideful because they would help her if she needed them. But like I said, her and her siblings had my Dad.

My mother said she knew her father, but she thought he was a white man living in a black neighborhood because he was married to a black woman. She later found out that his father was white and his mother was black and he always lived in the black community. She then realized that his mother was probably raped by a white man also.

When I think about the times they lived in I know it had to be hard on my grandmother Lillian. She was a tall black woman. My grandfather Jiles was also dark-skinned. When my mother Lenora was born she looked white with red hair and freckles. So, I know that my mother did not look like her parents or her siblings. When my grandmother was telling Mommy her story, she said that it never mattered that mother looked different; she was determined to love and nurture her and would never allow anyone to mistreat or abuse her.

It wasn't her fault how she was conceived. Mother was six years older than their next child but she says she never felt different, neglected or unwanted because her mother was such a kind loving person.

My grandmother Lillian had an Aunt Annie who lived to be one hundred and nine years old and we were very close. She loved to tell me stories about her niece, my grandmother. She always talked about how nice and compassionate she was. We never talked about my Mom's story though. I was fifteen when my Mom told me, but I don't think my mother ever discussed it with anyone else. I know that my Aunt Essie and my Uncle Lannie never mentioned it. I don't know if they knew.

My mother says her mother never allowed her or her siblings to spend the night with anyone until she got too sick to protect them anymore.

My mother never allowed my brother Milton or I to spend the night with anyone, either, until I was fourteen. My mother did not trust men with little girls or boys. Now, I don't trust women with little girls either. When I turned fourteen I had four best friends. Harriet, Ann, Gerry, and Rose. We were like joined at the hip. We went everywhere together. We dated in groups, because we were only looking for fun.

Harriett and Rose' parents never allowed them to spend the night with anyone. But Gerry, Ann, and I would take turns staying at each other's houses occasionally on weekends. The three of us slept in one bed. It never occurred to us to touch each other inappropriately. I don't know if we ever heard of the word homosexuality, but I know we never did anything to experiment with each other, even though we slept together. We also knew our place when it came to boyfriends and husbands. We were close, but we would step back whenever a boyfriend entered the picture. So, mother broke her rule about never spending the night when it came to Ann and Gerry. Because we traveled in a group, Mom trusted us and thought that provided a safety net, especially when it came to dating. It was also when she told me her story.

When I had my children, Mother went back to her rule. Do not leave your children with anyone but close relatives and make sure they can tell you everything, just in case Daddy, Uncle or Cousin lose their mind and make the mistake of touching you inappropriately.

I thank God for men like my father, George Drummond, who took my mother and her family in and loved, supported and provided for them with whatever they needed until he died.

Despite the hardships our parents and ancestors suffered, there was always some kind and loving person nearby to help.

My grandmother Lillian had two younger sisters who also died and left young children. My mother was the oldest of all of her first cousins, so she was always the matriarch in her family. Her and my father always kept their door open to relatives and friends who needed their help.

I now take my hat off to all of the slave women who bore children by their white masters. Some of these women were married and their husbands had to witness their wives being raped and then accept their white babies as their own.

But in most cases, they loved all of the children and protected them the best that they could under their circumstances in the village.

Many women are being raped today and some may have become pregnant.

To those who decide to keep their babies, I wish the blessings and strength of my grandmother, Lillian Pitts, on you.

Families go from faith to trials, to greater faith, to greater trials. It is a pilgrimage.

My Story Book starts with pictures of the people in my village when I was born and it ends with pictures of my village today.

I was named after my two grandmothers. My paternal grandmother was named Mary Drummond. My maternal grandmother was named Lillian Pitts. My name is Mary Lillian Drummond.

The following picture is of my paternal grandmother, Mary Drummond (left). She and my Aunt Sue (right) migrated from the cotton fields of South Carolina around 1930. My Aunt Sue and her husband, Henry, owned a barbershop, a beauty shop, and a restaurant. They bought a three-story house for other relatives who wanted to move north and get a new start. My mother and father moved to Philadelphia with them around 1935.

The Great Migration

My Parents going on their first flight in 1967.

George and Lenora Drummond were the first blacks to open a dry cleaning plant with sublet stores and laundry mats in Philadelphia in 1947.

Daddy said they built their houses, barns, schools, and churches in the South. Between planting, harvesting, and building, there wasn't much time for going to school. He stopped after the eight grade. I used to tease him and tell him he was an architectural engineer. It only took common sense.

Many African-Americans worked the cotton and tobacco fields or worked as live-in house servants in the South. They did not always have a formal education, but they were intelligent, with plenty of dignity and pride.

My mother's friend (left) migrated from the South to Philadelphia. She made hats and eventually opened a successful millinery shop.

This is a picture of my Uncle Lannie (right) and my cousin J.P. (left), who were both father figures to me. They reiterated everything daddy said. If I ever did anything to hurt or disappoint my parents, I had to answer to them and all the other relatives who were watching me.

Aunt Freddie and Uncle Lannie

Brother Milton, me, Mommy, and Delores (left to right). Her mother, Freddie, died giving birth to her and her father, Lannie, was away in World War II.

Uncle Lannie and his baby Delores. When this picture was taken, he was a single parent and had to raise his child alone.

The Picture on the left are brothers returning home to their families from World War II.

The Picture on the bottom are soldiers returning home from war, enjoying their war brides in Atlantic City.

Produce What You Consume

All of my parents' hats and dress clothing, as well as my little crinoline dresses, were custom made in the community.

This is my Uncle Lannie. He had a tailor in the neighborhood who made all of his dress clothes.

What Ghetto?

This is Cousin Roosevelt and Cousin Elizabeth's dining room. Some of the war brides stopped by for lunch. They had a large flower garden in their backyard. Neighbors would have their weddings and birthday parties in the yard, and then go inside their beautiful home for the reception. She was an event planner, but she was mostly known for her wedding cakes. Live musicians would play for her events.

Eight men in the family went to war. All of them returned home uninjured, mentally, and physically. Roosevelt (Ira) and his wife Elizabeth bought a house at 39th and Ogden St in West Philadelphia.

Father and Son

This is my first cousin, Willie, as a teenager in the 1940s. He is emulating his father, my Uncle Richard.

Our Parents were our first and most important role models.
This is a portrait of family pride and generational strength.

Life Has Come Full Circle

This is Delores with Uncle Lannie. The script got flipped and she became his caregiver. He had a massive stroke that left him paralyzed when he was 89 years old. This picture is a year later. He went and danced at his grandson's wedding. He lived to be 94 years old.

Aunt Essie "My Madea" at 89 years old.

She walked, talked, and looked like "Madea" when she was younger.

She taught us how to sing the blues with B.B. King, Lou Rawls, Fat's Domino, and others when we were down and feeling bad. We learned to express ourselves without degrading ourselves or others.

We could not go in the kitchen to cook without covering our street clothes with an apron. That was a stuffed pork roast and a duck on the table. She would sit in her chair and give us cooking instructions. Then we would set up her folding table before her and the family would sit down and eat with her on Sundays. This was her 89th birthday dinner. She died the next year at 90.

CHAPTER 1

LIFE IN THE VILLAGE

I was born in Philadelphia in 1941 to George and Lenora Drummond. I have one older brother, Arthur Milton Drummond, who was raised with me. My brother Milton was born after my parents were married fifteen years. I was born after nineteen years of marriage.

The village is formed:

I was born during World War II. My parents had bought a large three-story house. When the men in the family or a friend went off to war, their wives came to live with us. Our house was known as "The House of the War Brides."

There were seven cousins or friends who lived in our house during the time of the war. I called all of them auntie. My mother's sister-in-law, Freddie, lived with us. She became pregnant before Uncle Lannie left for the war and died days after my baby cousin Delores was born. My Uncle Lannie was on the front line in the war in Europe. The soldiers were not allowed to receive bad news from home and so he was not told until she was three months old and he was on his way home. He had nicknamed her "Cherry." She was well cared for after her mother died and her father was away at war because she had my mother, father, and seven aunts in the house to care and nurture her until her dad came home. Of course, this meant that my brother Milton and I had a baby sister in the house to look out for. She is now seventy years old, but she is still our baby sister. She still needs us to tell her what to do.

Children remember joy:

I remember the happy times when each of my relatives came home from the war. There would be tears of joy and lots of dinners and parties. I knew they were happy tears, so I was not upset or afraid.

I remember when the war was over. I was in the backyard with my mother. All of a sudden, people were running up and down the street dancing, hollering, crying, and saying that the war was over. Trolley's were clanking their bells, buses and cars were blowing their horns. People were getting out of their cars, hugging, and kissing strangers. There were a lot of tears, but I knew it was a happy time and I was not afraid.

Children remember trauma:

I also remember the trauma in my house when my Uncle Lannie returned home. I remember the fear and anxiety that I felt at that time and that it took a long time for me to recover. I guess it was because it took my family a long time to recover and I felt their sadness.

As I said above, my mother was not allowed to tell her brother Lannie that his wife Freddie had died in child birth, because his mail had been intercepted by navy officials. He was on his way home from the war when he received his bulk mail, telling him his wife had died. I was four years old and I was on the stairway going upstairs when all of a sudden my parents and my aunts who lived upstairs were running down the steps, screaming and hollering. The door opened and a man walked in wearing a white uniform. He fell in the floor crying and all of my family was rolling on the floor crying.

Angry with God:

After a while, he sat down on the sofa, and Mommy handed him his four-month-old daughter, Delores. He then realized that he was a single parent with a newborn baby to raise. My mother said he was very depressed for a long time and angry with God. He said he could not understand how she could die in childbirth with doctors all around her, when he saw soldiers with their limbs blown off live.

I would not go near him for a long time because I did not like this man who caused so much pain and crying in my house.

He rented an apartment in my parent's house for him and Delores and they lived there until she was seven years old. That's when he remarried. His wife had three children. So, I witnessed him as a stepfather and her children loved him dearly. They had one daughter together, Penny. They divorced when their daughter was fourteen years old and he raised their daughter alone as a single parent.

Therefore, I already knew the responsibilities of a single parent because I had him and other members in my village who walked before me and let me see that it could be done.

Family historian:

One friend of the family, who was a war bride and lived in our house, Aunt Hazel, is still living. She is 94 years old and Aunt Freddie was her sister. She has never owned a car. She walks and rides public transportation everywhere she goes. She jumps rope and rides her stationary bike every day. She is still a trustee in her church. She's the organist and the janitor. They now only allow her to dust. She still works as a volunteer in the emergency room of Bryn Mawr hospital where she retired from more than 25 years ago.

She has traveled extensively around the world. It is delightful to talk to her because she has led a full life in front of me, despite the tragedies in her life. I have watched her bounce back from many situations. I'm glad I have kept her in my circle of friends because there is an intergenerational spirit needed to survive in the village

My oldest brother:

My father had an older son named Ben. He was born in Pennsylvania Hospital in Philadelphia in 1929. His mother named him Benjamin Franklin and he grew up to be a great pharmacist.

She was not able to keep him, but she had a great vision for his life. He lived with many different family members in his own village, but he said that each guardian loved and strengthened him to go on and make great strides in his life. Even though his mother was not with him, she stayed in contact with him (that would be like open adoption today). The only work women could find in the 1920s was as a live-in maid, so that's what she did. He got in a little trouble when he was fifteen years old and she was afraid that he was getting on the wrong track.

His mother moved him from Woodruff, South Carolina to Columbus, Ohio. She placed him in a boarding home near her job. She put him in school there and visited him on her day off. She watched him closely and encouraged him to get a good education. He went to Howard University and became a Pharmacist.

He became the first black man to serve as a hospital administrator over the Department of Pharmacy in Columbus, Ohio. He was a member of the National Alliance of Black Pharmacists, Alpha Phi Alpha Fraternity and received many honorary doctorate degrees for the contributions he made to healthcare. All of these organizations have a great history to tell about his life and service to others. He served as a Deacon, choir member and Sunday school teacher in his church. He also established a prison ministry and a ministry for bereaved families.

In the 1960s, when the black professionals in Columbus, Ohio were ready to build or buy their own homes, they were not wanted in white communities. They organized and bought a large tract of land and developed their own community. They selected land across the street from a house that served as an underground railroad for slaves in route to Canada. My brother and others traced their history in that area back to the 1800s. They wanted a reminder of how far they had come as a people.

Talking to a Dying Christian

When he was diagnosed with cancer we started talking about what it will be like to be in the in the presence of God. There will be no need for a Sun, because God's Glory will be shinning so bright.

Christians will be coming from every nation, singing and playing harps. A number no man can count.

He died January 30, 2014. He was truly my best friend.

His pastor said in his eulogy:

"We are crying because we miss him, but don't cry for him because this was his goal in life. He worked towards this day. All he wanted was to be fit and accepted in God's Kingdom."

"I press toward the goal to win the prize for which God has called me heavenward in Christ Jesus" (Phil. 3:14).

CHAPTER 2

THE EXTENDED FAMILY
WITHIN THE VILLAGE

My father had eleven brothers and sisters, and so, I had many first cousins, male and female. I was the youngest of all of the Drummond grandchildren in Philadelphia. This gave me a very special place in the family. I had many mentors to love, support and guide me. When they started having their own children I was naturally their first babysitter. This also meant that I had a lot of little cousins looking up to me for love, support and guidance. I am now the matriarch of the family because most of their parents have passed away. My cousin Lauren Brewton is doing a genealogy on our family and I am the historian for her research.

Significance of First Cousins:

There's just nothing like the relationship that you have with your first cousins. They know everything about you. They know your parents' secrets, even events that happened in the family before you were born that had a direct influence on your life that you knew nothing about. There are always a few who love to tell your true story, but the majority will take certain information with them to their grave.

But, as each of us started to lose our parents it was our first cousins who would sit with us in the hospital all night long. Cousins will hold you, cry with you and help you say good bye. You don't have to talk much or try to tell them how you feel because they already know. We all walked with each other as our parents were lowered in the ground. I walked with their children as each one of them was buried. In silence, there was no need for words. There are only three of us left now from my father's generation living in Philadelphia, my cousin, Sue, and my brother, Milton.

My father had one brother, Miles Drummond, who has children living in Cincinnati, Ohio.

CHAPTER 3

NEIGHBORS IN THE VILLAGE

There were seven children living next door to us when I was born, five girls and two boys. They were all my mentors. I remember when I started kindergarten, Mildred and Connie would be on either side of me, holding my hands and walking me to school.

When I was fourteen years old I lit a cigarette in front of their brother Buddy. He slapped it right out of my hand, he said, "Oh no! You are not going to start that." He was eighteen years old.

A true friend wants the best for you and they do not want to see you form any bad habits that will harm you.

They were at my side when I lost my parents. I understood their grief when they lost their parents and three of their siblings at an early age.

I've attended their family reunions from Philadelphia to Colorado. Recently, the oldest sister, Leona, celebrated her eightieth birthday. It felt so good to be with friends who have known me since birth. I don't have to tell them anything about myself. They know my story because they have witnessed every stage of my life.

When we travel together by bus or plane, we sometimes ride in silence. I already know what's going on currently in their life and they know what I'm thinking and feeling. We know what life experiences have shaped our character and personality and why we respond to certain situations the way we do. I have never really had the need for a psychologist. I learned from family and next door neighbors the importance and significance of family and friends befrore I started school. I walked away from every school, job and neighborhood with at least one life time friend.

CHAPTER 4

GHETTO, WHAT GHETTO?

Sometimes when I meet people and tell them where I grew up, they will say, "Oh, you're from the hood, the ghetto or from down the bottom." I ask myself, "bottom of what?" In the 1940s, we lived on tree line streets. Our houses had hardwood floors, French doors, crystal chandeliers, and large mirrors trimmed with gold frames. We had custom made satin brocade drapes that were lined and matching slip-covers on our furniture.

On Sundays, we set our tables with lace tablecloths, beautiful Chinaware, pure silverware, crystal glasses, and linen napkins.

My mother and all of my aunts wore mink coats and my father bought a new Buick every four years.

There were seven children and four adults who lived next door to me. There were ten children and two adults in the third house from mine. I never went into any of my neighbor's houses and found anything out of place. Their houses were always clean, neat, well furnished and organized. If there was any dysfunction in their homes, it was not obvious.

The GI Bill:

When the men in my family returned home from the war, they bought houses in the community on the G.I. Bill. I had a relative on every corner and their houses looked just like mine. My cousins Elizabeth and Roosevelt's house had a large flower garden. She was a caterer and an event planner. Neighbors would have their weddings and parties in her garden and the receptions in her gorgeous house.

Cousin Elizabeth had friends who were musicians and they would come and provide live entertainment when she was having an affair in her home. Almost every one had a piano in their house. When visitors would come, one of their children would play and another would sing to entertain you.

The GI Bill also provided the soldiers coming home from the war with scholarships to college. It elevated the life of many blacks who used this opportunity to go to college and become lawyers, doctors, engineers, and other professions that we could not have had access to previously.

Years later, my oldest brother Ben went into the service and used the GI Bill to go to college and become a pharmacist.

After the war brides moved out, relatives from the south would come to stay with us until they could find a job, and then they would move out and another set of relatives or friends would move in until they could get a new start.

Subsidized housing:

After the influx of my family migrating from the South passed, my parents started renting to singles and families. Many of them could not afford to pay rent at the market rate because so many jobs had left the city. So, my parents charged them according to their income or they would have been homeless. This was subsidized housing before the government started low-income housing or the projects. Many of our neighbors who had large houses did the same thing. The village took care of their own problems and helped people in whatever way they needed help.

We knew that some of them had mental problems and problems with alcohol. But my father would say, "Take your nonsense outside. This is a place of peace. It is your sanctuary; you don't have to act like that in here." There was no medication or AA groups to attend, but they would talk and listen to my parents. My parents theme in life was "If I can help somebody along the way then my living will not be in vain."

Funerals in the home:

I heard my parents talk about people being funeralized in their home. I witnessed this two times. One of my childhood friends lost her father and he was laid out in their living room. I remember one of them holding me up to see their father in the coffin.

There was a white family in the neighborhood who had five children. They had one daughter about four years old, who was hit by a car in front of their house. She was funeralized at home. The whole black community came out and supported the family with finances and food. As stated above, neighbors came together and helped people in whatever way help was needed.

CHAPTER 5

GUNS, GANGS AND MOTHERS

The 1970s is when you can really start to see the change in families. I heard Andrew Young, who was Mayor of Atlanta at the time, say, "We have progressed to split-level houses and split-level families." Broken homes have caused poor communication and serious breakdowns in our families, rich and poor alike.

My father and every other member of my family had guns in their houses. My brother and I knew where my parents kept their guns, but I never knew of or heard a story about a child who ever touched his parents' gun. All of the men in my family had their service revolvers from World War II. My parents said that they kept their shotguns over their front door at all times in the South.

Families were intact; they had respect for their parents, and each other. In the summertime, we could sleep on the porch at night in our night clothes with our doors open.

Gangs and Mothers:
In the 1960s, the gangs were so out of control that teenage boys could not walk from one neighborhood to another without crossing into another turf and being killed by rival gangs.

I had a cousin, Blanch Nixon, who had six children. She heard a rumor that her second son, Norman, belonged to a gang. She didn't believe it because she was so active in the community with the youth, she thought he would know better. She kept her ears and eyes open listening to conversations in the community. Then she started listening in on his phone calls because he was denying his involvement.

One night, she heard a phone call telling him to meet them at 58th and Cedar Avenue to fight the Cedar Avenue gang. She knew the mothers of her sons' friends. She called them and told them to meet her at the corner of 58th and Cedar. When the boys arrived at the corner they looked up and saw their mothers coming down the street also. They said they would have to come through them before they could fight each other. They contacted mothers of other gang members across the City and formed a mothers club. They reduced the number of gang members being murder in Philadelphia tremendously.

When graffiti was getting totally out of control, Blanche Nixon contacted the library at 58th and Baltimore Avenue in Philadelphia. She organized the young graffiti artists and let them draw and display their art on the library wall. That was the very first mural that went up in the City of Philadelphia. She then went to the Philadelphia Electric Company and raised funds for graffiti artists to paint a mural. It was hung in the subway station at 22nd and Market Street around 1968.

Norman, along with many of his gang member friends, went into the military service after graduating from High School, not jail. When they returned home from the service, she got them to join her organization to fight against crime and gangs in the community. They went on to write a proposal to the City Police Department's Gang Control Division. They were funded because they knew the families in the neighborhood involved in criminal activity. Benny Swanns became the first Director of Crisis Intervention and Blanch Nixon became the President of the Board of Directors. When she died, City Council named the library at 58th and Cobbs Creek Parkway in South West Philadelphia, the Blanch Nixon Library.

Homeless but Hopeful

I was a social worker for the Office of Emergency Shelter and Services in 1990 when one case came across my desk that I'll never forget.

I worked as a Coordinator for Transitional Housing. I helped mothers develop a plan to move out of the shelter for the homeless. Savings was the key element. I used realtors who were concerned and willing to give parents with poor credit a chance to rent their houses or apartments.

I had a client named Pat. She found a new job and saved enough to rent a house and move up and out of shelter. She had four children. I made an appointment for her with a realtor who participated in our program by renting to our clients. The appointment was set for 11:00 a.m. on a Wednesday morning. The realtor called me from the property saying she never showed up, she didn't call the realtor, me or tell the shelter manager where she was going. I got so angry I told the realtor to forget her because I had another client who was ready to rent her house. The next morning, she came to my office begging for another chance.

This is her story:

She was ready to go to her appointment to see the house when an old neighbor showed up at the shelter. The neighbor told Pat that her eleven-year-old son, Tim, had helped some of the boys in the old neighborhood rob a house. When Pat asked Tim what happened and why, he said, "the gang threatened to beat me up if I didn't help them." There was a house on their old block that was sitting empty because the couple had died. The gang chose Tim because he was little for an eleven year old. They held him up and put him through the narrow bathroom window. He then opened the door for them and they cleaned the house out. Pat took her son to the police and made him give the name of every boy involved. They went to each child's house and recovered most of everything stolen. She got a friend to drive the furniture back to the house. She made her son move furniture and appliances from the curb into the house by himself and set the house up like it was, and then she paid a locksmith to put on new locks. When they got back to the shelter, she took him outside and beat him as hard as she could. She told her son that she was going to be worse than any gang he could ever meet. If he was going to be afraid of anybody in this world, it should be her, and whenever he has a problem in life he should come to her first.

She told him, "I have four children and a chance to move out of the shelter. When I walk through the door of our next house I will have four children walking in behind me, not three."

I put Pat in a city car and drove her to the realtor's office and we begged him for another chance.She rented her new house in a new neighborhood that day.

Reputation is important. Pat was poor and struggling, but her neighbors knew her reputation and knew she wanted the best for her children, so they went out of their way to find her.

Mothers, take charge, eliminate as many negative messages from television, social media, music, and friends from your child's culture as you can. Give them hope. If what they are doing does not please God, then it shouldn't please them either, avoid it.

CHAPTER 6

ENTREPRENEURS

Many of my family members, who moved from the south as farmers, started their own businesses when they came to Philadelphia. My father's brothers and sisters owned beauty and barbershops, restaurants, and daycare facilities. My father worked as a maintenance man in the Earl Theater. Black entertainers would come to perform at the theater, but they could not stay in the white hotels downtown. My Aunt Hannah bought a three story house. My father would refer the entertainers to her house. The first floor was a restaurant and she rented the rooms on the second and the third floors to travelers.

In 1947, my mother and father were the first blacks to own a dry cleaning plant in Philadelphia. There was a bank owned by a black man called The Lincoln Bank at 18th and South Street. The bank closed at 3 p.m., and that was the busiest time of day for my mother and father in their cleaners.

Black people would travel across the city to patronize black businesses. When I was around ten years old, my mother would dress me up in pretty, wide crinoline dresses, with Shirley temple curls and patent leather shoes. They would strap bags of money on me under my crinoline slips. Mom would put me on the 40 bus and place me behind the same bus driver every day at about 2 p.m. My Aunt Sue owned a beauty salon, barbershop, and a restaurant at 17th and South Street. When I would get off the bus, she would be waiting for me. She would take me to a room in the back of the Lincoln Bank and take the bags of money off of me. She would deposit my father's money in the bank and then take me to lunch in the restaurant that she owned. This was my special time with her every day. I would stay with her until daddy closed the cleaners and picked me up.

CHAPTER 7

THE WAR BOOST THE ECONOMY

My father worked for the Sun Ship Yard during World War II. He was a welder building ships for the war. He earned enough money to take care of his family. He saved enough money to open his own business by the time the war was over.

My parents only went to the eighth grade in school, but they were very intelligent people. Daddy had to tear out the existing walls and ceilings in the garage of the three story building he purchased. They had to be built within certain dimensions to hold the heavy cleaning machinery and pressers for the business. Daddy did it all. One day when I came home from school Daddy was down in this deep dark hole digging the dirt out, so it could be ready to pour the new cement.

He looked up at me and said, "Baby, I'm doing this for you." When I got older I asked him how he knew how to do it? He said, "We built everything we needed in the south, houses, barns, churches, and schools. I went to his brother's house in Spartanburg, South Carolina as a child. He had a large house with a porch that ran all around the house. Daddy said that he and his brothers built that house.

Daddy's favorite saying was, "Mr. Need is a bad man, but Mr. Got To Have will make you think there is nothing you cannot do."

Produce what you consume:

The answer to our problems today is opportunity. In my time during the forties, fifties, and part of the sixties, the United States produced what they consumed. Every adult that I knew who wasn't sick went to work. Blacks worked in factories making supplies for the Armed Services, and bicycles, wedding gowns, children's clothing, canned goods, paper goods, steel mills, lumber mills and all of the building trades.

High schools were open at night for adults. You could get a high school diploma, take instructions, and be tutored for government tests for city, state, and federal jobs. You could learn trades like typing, shorthand, telephone operator, millinery, shoe repair, dress-making, and tailoring. Men could go to school and learn all of the building trades. Industries came into the high schools, such as Westinghouse, and taught the boys drafting and tool and dye making. Then they hired them when they graduated. When we were an Industrial Society there was work for everyone. When factories closed and people lost their jobs, they built low income housing projects and offered welfare to families. This had its good and bad sides because many families who could no longer find work or housing were starving.

The government eroded their own tax base but this was still considered cheaper than paying everyone a living wage. Corporations preferred moving to India or China where they can get eight employees to work for the price of one in the United States. For instance, Comcast service technicians can fix your cable television and internet problems and some of them are in the Philippines. They are exploiting the poor in foreign countries because they do not provide a living wage, benefits, or a safe work environment. Everything needed for the recent wars has been made in foreign countries and gone into the pockets of conglomerates, such as Halliburton Industries. War does not boost our economy anymore; it only makes the rich man richer and the poor man poorer.

Our men die for the cause, but they do not benefit from it. There are stories out now about the poor medical care that veterans receive due to lack of funding. Somebody got funded.

Minimum wage:

Now, there is a call to raise the minimum wage in the United States. One congressman said, "This should not be because it will cause corporations to lose their bottom line." In other words, they will lose their profit margin. He said, "And they will only layoff more people and continue outsourcing."

Another congressman said, "Unemployment should not be extended because it's making people think they are entitled to unemployment and not taking the jobs that are available." Congressmen do not acknowledge that all working employees pay into the unemployment fund. Therefore, the unemployment fund should not be depleted. They want workers who made a living wage for twenty or more years of working to now accept jobs for minimum wage.

The attitude in Congress now is that we should not feel entitled to any benefits, health benefits, housing, or welfare. It has been suggested that children should work for their lunches. A congressman said that, "We're sending school children the wrong message regarding entitlements. They should learn that you cannot get anything in this world free." People who cannot find jobs that pay a living wage are considered lazy.

Pay check to pay check:

The answer was every child should go to college. I went to college in 1976, after I graduated I got a job as a medical social worker. I only made $10,000 a year, which did not cover my bills. I made $10,000 a year in 1963 as a comptometer operator. I had to work a part-time job at night and weekends to pay my bills and take care of my two children. I did eventually move up the pay scale to earn a decent living. I guess I would have been considered lower middle class.

There are college graduates today that work at banks and other corporations that only earn $10 an hour. A member services representative in a bank, providing loans for the customers are only making a few dollars above minimum wage. Corporations now have something called, "at will employment," which gives them the right to fire an employee without justification or a process for appeal. If there is any attempt to join a union, the corporations have the right to fire you. These policies are taking us back to the days before unions were formed.

There are many students who owe between forty thousand dollars and a hundred thousand dollars in student loans. They have to live at home until this debt is paid because this will affect their credit rating and keep them from renting an apartment, buying a car, or a house. There are many jobs that will check your credit rating and if it is poor or you owe any money on your student loans you cannot get the job.

Economics is always the major factor affecting the welfare and well-being of the village. There are people in their fifties losing their jobs and their houses and moving back home with their parents who are senior citizens. In some cases, it's good for everyone because their parents' income is not meeting all of their expenses today either. Families really need each other to survive in the village once again.

Industrial Revolution: Opportunity

My father-in-law, Albert, was born July 4, 1921. When he was four years old, trucks came into his town in Virginia. They moved families to Clearfield, Pennsylvania. When they arrived, they moved into two- and three-bedroom row houses. His father went to work in a tile factory and they were no longer destitute. Some of the men in the community became long-distance truck drivers, delivering floor tiles to stores across the country. They earned a very good living and their sons looked forward to finishing high school and traveling across the country like their fathers. They had wonderful stories to tell about the things they saw and the difference in how people lived. Their community thrived, even though they were segregated. The village was self-sufficient and they owned their own homes and businesses.

My father-in-law finished high school shortly before World War II started. He went into the service and learned to be a chef. When he came home, he became a chef for Penn State University. He worked there until he retired. Jobs were stable and provided lifetime security.

Good old times: Respect

There were some good old times back in the day when people had trades and skills that helped them provide for their families. My girlfriend Nellie had nine children, one daughter, and eight sons. Her husband Willie died suddenly of a heart attack. Nellie worked in a factory that made women's clothes. She earned a living wage and she was able to provide all of the necessities for her children, even though her husband had died.

This is so important; her children did not feel desperate or destitute because they had lost their dad. The boys got little jobs in the community to buy the extra things they wanted, but having the kind of security that they had at home left them room to be creative. They bought musical instruments and taught themselves to sing and dance. It was a good time house.

Another thing the parents had instilled in their children was a chain of command. Each child was responsible for the next child under them. They had to know where each other was at all times because the parents spent a lot of time away from home working. Each child looked up to the older ones with respect and they did not want to do anything that would bring shame to the Smith family. These values and standards were in place before the father died.

When the older brothers started graduating from high school, they didn't have the money for all of the things they wanted for the prom. When each of her sons and her daughter went to their prom, she made their tuxedos and evening gowns with matching capes. The word spread throughout the neighborhood and she was eventually making evening clothes for the whole community, wedding gowns included.

Then the young people in the community said they wanted an opportunity to wear their clothes more than once. Nellie's children were self taught musicians and singers. So they started renting halls and giving fashion shows and dinner dances. Nellie would make trunks for the men and matching bathing suits for the girls, so that couples could model together.

My mother, who never went into a nightclub or dance hall in her whole life, started going to their parties. She would put on her Sunday hat, pocketbook, and gloves, and dance in her chair all night long. She knew that the Smith children had never taken formal music lessons in their life. She said it tickled her to her toes to see the Smith children perform. Nellie had a reputation for her food throughout the neighborhood. So, when the word got out that the Smith family was having a party, old neighbors came back from everywhere to join the fun. They knew it would be safe, clean fun. No one ever got drunk or caused any commotion; they had too much respect for Mrs. Smith and her children.

One of her sons, Jeffrey, started a limousine service, which he still owns today. Another son, Danny, became an auto mechanic for Toyota. Seven of Nellie's children owned Toyotas. On Sundays when all of the children would come home for dinner, Toyota cars would stretch down the entire block. So, we were always styling and profiling and riding first-class to their social events.

The Smith brothers eventually opened the Smith brother's auto parts store.

Nellie now has a picnic in the park on the first Saturday of July for all of her children, grandchildren, great-grandchildren, family, and friends. More than a hundred people attend. There's no fighting or disrespect because she is held in such high esteem by everyone who knows her. We just have a good time like the good old days.

It was easier for families to survive tragedies in their life when they have skills and trades to sustain them. Lost Arts: So many of the trades, skills, and arts that we used to use to survive have been lost. When people don't produce what they consume it takes away their pride, their feeling of belonging and it robs them of energy and creativity.

CHAPTER 8

THE CULTURE OF POVERTY/
THE CULTURE OF CONGRESS

It is important to understand the culture of poverty in the village. There are approximately three categories of poverty: chronic, situational, and generational.

Chronic poverty:

Individuals, head of households, or family members who are disabled due to physical or mental illness. These persons will need permanent help, not because they are lazy or crazy, but because they are sick. They still need affordable housing, a monthly income that will allow them to live with dignity, and access to medical care.

Situational poverty:

The working poor and the unemployed make up the largest percentage of people living in poverty. Many professional jobs are being watered down or eliminated. So we have people with college degrees working for minimum wage and their lifestyle is chronic, also. Their situation can last from six months to sixteen years, which was my situation. After finishing college, I did eventually move up and out of the situation of living hand to mouth or pay check to pay check, but so much damage had been done in the interim that it took years to repair. Especially when it came to my house. There was a great deal of structural repairs needed on my home that I could not afford before. So, all of those areas of neglect had to be addressed.

Even though I was working, I couldn't afford Christmas. When my children were little I would start right after Christmas, buying a toy now and then so they would have something under the tree. By the time my children were teenagers I was so poor we didn't bother buying a tree because there wasn't anything to put under it. I told my children, "If you flick the switch and the lights come on,

Merry Christmas." We didn't cry, complain, or tell our family members because my mortgage and utilities were paid and we had all of the food and clothing necessary to be comfortable, just nothing extra.

Generational poverty:

People who live in poverty, stuck in subsidized housing, and on welfare for generation after generation. They have lost hope because they have no vision. Sickness or the lost of a job that paid a living wage may have plunged the head of a household into a deplorable living situation and many other problems kept them there. So, the next generation grew up under these impoverish conditions. If they are surrounded by people who are poor spiritually, financially, and emotionally, then no one has anything to give. They don't know the way up and out of their situation and this mindset is passed down from one generation to the next.

The difference between me, who lived in situational poverty and those who live in generational poverty is the fact that I wasn't born into poverty.

My parents provided a beautiful, comfortable life for me as a child. When I got married I lived a very beautiful and comfortable life until the age of thirty. Sometimes when I was really struggling I would look back and say, well I didn't know what it was like to have a problem until I reached the age of thirty. Then I became a single mother with two children, a mortgage, and no job.

I didn't think I had the right to complain because I know that everyone is going to have a cross of some kind to bear before they leave this world. I was about the poorest person I knew within my familial village. Being poor however, did not have anything to do with my faith, my values, my morals, my pride, or my expectations. All of that was in place before I became poor.

My children always looked nice when they went out. They had manners and were respectful. You could not just look at us and tell that things were bad. I had so much love and support from family and friends that I knew that one day things would change for the better.

The Culture of Congress:

The members of Congress, who are paid with our tax dollars, make the decisions as to who should live a healthy lifestyle. Their minimum wage is $170,000 a year, but they think that $7.25 per hour is sufficient for the working class. They say that their constituents are always begging. "The more you give them, the more they want." "Why should all people feel entitled to jobs that pay a living wage, affordable housing, and healthcare?"

They are proposing a 3.3 trillion dollar cut in funds for social services, but 614 billion dollars have been proposed for corporate welfare. So executives of failing businesses can still get their salaries plus bonuses.

Congressional hearings are being held and research conducted to study the needs of the poor. If some people are making $12,000 per year and you are making $170,000 a year, how much more research is needed?

Congress works with corporations to privatize government jobs and services. Most of these new corporations that are emerging are establishing their own pay scales, policies and benefits. They are also prohibiting the employees from joining unions.

The government contracts out and privatize services like education, health care, social services, to name a few. But the employees won't have the pensions and benefits that we had when we worked for the government directly.

Disparity: The Urban League Unveiled a Report On Black America

In the Philadelphia Tribune on March 20, 2015.

"Median income for blacks in the Philadelphia metropolitan area (which includes Philadelphia, Camden, NJ and Wilmington, DE) is about $36,802 in comparison to $71,916 for whites.

The index used to study the job crisis, education crisis and a justice crisis shows the history of race in America has created advantages for whites that persist in many of the outcomes being measured."

Drug Dealing

With legal jobs eroding, drug dealing substitutes employment. We cannot get information on how to open variety stores, clothing stores, or shoe stores in our community, but information is flowing on how to get shipments of drugs to come into our village. The system is designed to provide destructive, rather than constructive, energy into our village.

Slavery Today:

President Obama stated in his 2015 State of The Union address that "the minimum wage should be raised to $15.00 an hour." He said, "if you think this is too high, then you, the Congress, should try living on it.

I agree with him, but in the real world it will hurt us in the long run.

The United States are invested in countries that are engaged in slavery or slave wages. Our furs, diamonds, rubber, oil, clothing ,leather and ivory, to name a few, made for the United States by corporations they own in poor countries and imported to the United States. The fishing industries in India and parts of Ghana use slave labor, including children, and this seafood is shipped to the largest food chains in America.

And so, although I agree with President Obama, I am afraid that an increase in "outsourcing" will be Corporate America's response to paying workers a living wage in the United States.

Slavery is alive and well around the world.

Unions VS Institutional Racism:

Unions are our best resource when voting for new politicians. Unions have the most experience when it comes to following a potential politicians track record.

They have meetings for members and retirees and newsletters to keep us abreast of current issues. They know which candidates come into our communities telling us what we want to hear, but vote differently when they get into office. We still need unions, but unions need to strategize and come up with ways to fight these new corporations emerging who block them out. We need their protection because corporations are now instituting policies that take us back to days before unions were formed. It's called "Institutional racism."

CHAPTER 9

HOPE

The Philadelphia Tribune, Tues., Oct. 28, 2014

"With opportunity gaps widening for poor children and children of color, new guidance from the Office for Civil Rights in the U.S. Department of Education offers new hope and protection from discrimination. States, school districts and schools must make education resources equally available to all students regardless to race, color or national origin."

Hats off to:

Marian Wright Edelman, President of the Children's Defense Fund, whose "Leave No Child Behind" mission is to ensure every child a Healthy Start, a Head Start, a Fair Start, and a Moral Start in life and a successful passage to adulthood with the help of caring families and communities.

The STEM program: That's our future

The STEM program (Science, Technology, Engineering, and Math) is being incorporated into our educational curriculums from preschool through college.

Our leaders in education are realizing that the United States will not be able to compete with other industrialized nations. We must increase our children's skills in the STEM areas.

The Obama administration has challenged colleges and universities to graduate 1 million students through STEM over the next ten years.

Jamie Bracey, a black woman and Director at Temple University STEM education, is bringing diversity to the field. She understands the importance of global connectivity by networking with others around the world.

But she also knows that children of color are coming out of schools that have given them an inflated sense of preparation. "They'll have an 'A' average, but they have not had the curriculum in science and math to sustain them in a rigorous academic program."

I'm glad that the STEM program is being included in preschool programs. My great grandchildren attended one at the ages of three and five and they now know how to build a robot that can forecast a hurricane, earthquake, or tornado. Yes, they can learn. Thanks to Mr. Tariq Al-Nisar at Harambe Institute in Philadelphia, their STEM teacher, who believed that children should start learning science at three years old.

New Employment for Women, Fox 5 NEWS, NY, Sat., Jan. 3, 2015:

This documentary showed the explosion of women in nontraditional jobs, such as construction and manufacturing.

Small Businesses:

There are small business administrations in every state. They will help you with your business ideas and how to bring them to fruition.

Opportunities Industrialization Center of Philadelphia:

Opportunities Industrialization Center of Philadelphia (OIC), founded by Dr. Leon Sullivan, evolved into a national and international education and training program. They have helped more than 3 million people worldwide to learn trades and establish their own businesses and they are still here to help you.

Two current organizations: We're still rising

The Philadelphia Tribune, www.Phillytrib.com, Friday, October 16, 2015, by Ayana Jones, reported: Shalimar Thomas, a young black woman, just resigned as Executive Director of the African American Chamber of Commerce of Pennsylvania, New Jersey and Delaware.

She is now the Executive Director of the North Broad Street Renaissance, a nonprofit created to promote community economic development, historic preservation and arts and culture along the North Broad Street Corridor.

"WITHOUT A VISION PEOPLE PERISH"

CHAPTER 10

WHAT HAPPENED TO BLACK ENTREPRENEURS?

Well, I'll start with my family. I said under the title motivations that I can identify with the T.V. show *Sweetie Pie*. Business ownership is exhausting and time consuming. My father and most of his siblings owned their own businesses. All of their time and energy was spent working nights and weekends, when everyone else was off. It robbed them of family time and it took all of their creative energy to stay open, alert to competition, and changing economic trends.

I laugh when I watch the T.V. show *Sweetie Pie* because their son Tim reminds me of my father; he is always looking for another venue. He's always running to start a new restaurant. My father was always looking for the opportunity to open another location for his sublet dry cleaning stores or laundry mats.

My father did devote Sundays to his family, he took us to church. It didn't matter how late my brother stayed out at night my father would be at the door when he came in and say "be ready for church on time." Plus, we worked in the cleaners and we could go to his job to spend time with him when we wanted to because he owned it. But my mother said, "The only thing he thinks about is that cleaners." However, I never felt neglected by my dad. But , my mother, aunts, and uncles did not prepare or encourage any of their children to take over their businesses. They encouraged all of their children to go to college or take a government job. They wanted us to work forty-hour shifts, have security, earn a living wage, have benefits, and have time for our families.

I tried to hold onto my father's dry cleaning business until 1977, but there were so many changes taking place and affecting the industry. Wash and wear materials were a large hit, the modernization of equipment, and the change in cleaning fluids. The layout of the plant stretched two blocks and required the employment of several employees. The machinery was so outdated that there weren't many mechanics left to fix or maintain the machinery.

So, whenever you are in business you must be ready to handle the fluctuating trends that will change your mode of operation.

I was not ready to make the gross changes that were needed to survive in the industry. I felt bad about it because I wanted to hold on to the family business my father worked so hard to establish, but my children and I were suffering. I finally came to the conclusion that my father loved me more than he loved the business. He would not want me to have a nervous breakdown worrying about the business. I finally got the courage to close the business in 1977 and go to school.

Of course, during this time large corporations were emerging and making it almost impossible for small businesses to survive anyway.

The manufacturing conglomerates which moved to foreign countries also made it possible for the wholesaler and retailer there to move to the United States and sell the products that are manufactured in their country. They took over every business district in every community in the United States.

Fortune 500 companies own almost every aspect of the business world.

We moved from an industrial society to a service society, but that's not even true now because many of the service or marketing jobs have been moved to foreign countries also. If you call Comcast cable for service, you may get a service technician in India or the Philippines. However, I don't understand their accent, so it takes a long time to understand their answers or instructions for solving a technical problem over the phone.

The system we live in today will break your leg and then blame you for limping.

The system will steal your livelihood and then call you lazy.

The system will break your spirit and call you crazy.

If you let it.

CHAPTER 11

FAMILY AND FRIENDS WILL HELP YOU

As a single parent, I had to learn how to accept help. I met my friend Harriet Norman in kindergarten. We were fourteen when we met Gerry, Ann, and Rose. The five of us were inseparable. We were in each other's weddings and we are the godparents to each other's children. We lost two out of our circle: Harriet and Rose. But we loved, supported, and stayed with each other until the circle was broken. The three of us who are left continue to stick together through thick and thin: Ann, Gerry, and I.

When Harriet got married she moved to California, but distance didn't make a difference between us. She could always sense when something was wrong with one of us back home.

Trouble In The Air:

My husband and I were married three years before our son Damon was born. I wanted to make sure we had a solid marriage before having children. I was determined not to have children caught in the middle of separation and divorce.

Well, of course I learned that there's no such thing as a guarantee. It doesn't matter how good things look they can change for the worst. It doesn't matter how bad things are they can get better.

My husband and I separated after eight years of marriage. We had two children: Damon, age five and Kenya, age two. After I closed the dry cleaning plant, I decided to go back to school. The children were six and nine years old. I was a single parent, working part-time and going to school full-time.

One day as I was parking my car, a couple who lived across the street pulled up and parked behind me. I had been seeing them and waving hello for about six months, but I never knew their names.

The wife jumped out of her car and ran up to me, accusing me of going with her husband. She raised her fist to punch me, but her husband grabbed her arm and dragged her across the street. I was so shocked that I just stood there frozen for a few minutes.

When I walked into my house in a daze the phone rang. It was my girlfriend Harriet from California. She asked "What's wrong?" Now this was perfect because she knows me well enough to know that I would never go with anyone's husband. I didn't have to say that.

She knew everything I was going through and how I was struggling with how much help I would accept from my family, my in-laws, and my friends. My husband left and I felt the responsibility was mine alone. I was determined not to lean on other people. Not because of too much pride, but because I was afraid that something big would happen, like the heater or the roof would need fixing and I would have to ask for help. I didn't want to drain them dry before an emergency came up. Harriet just talked to me about letting the friends and family in my village help me financially as well as emotionally.

When I got married in 1963, I was a comptometer operator (this was before computers). I earned $10,000 a year. My husband was a plain clothes detective earning $20,000. I was ready to start my family in 1966, so I stopped work, but we bought a duplex. The apartment on the second floor brought in $6,000 a year and he was then making $24,000, so I still had an income of $30,000.

After my husband quit his job and left home, I went from an income of $30,000 a year to $6,000 a year. I closed my dry cleaning business because I wasn't making any money. I started working part-time, going to school full-time at night and doing my internship for social work at Children's Hospital.

I was traveling by trolley to school and work when Septa went on strike. The night before the strike started, my cousin J.P. showed up with an old raggedy car. He said you have to take this car to keep going. I said, "I can't afford the insurance." He said, "I'm paying it on mine right now." The strike lasted about six months, so I was really grateful that I had a car. But I knew my mother was ashamed of my riding in such a bad-looking car and of course she was afraid it would break down on me with the children in the car at night. So Harriet reminded me that I have a lot of people to help me and I needed to be more receptive to help.

The day after the woman across the street threatened to get me, I came outside and all of my windows had been broken out of my car. All I could think about was the fact that I didn't have a car to get to school or work. I was so devastated I just collapsed on the sidewalk. No one came by and I don't know how long I laid there before I crawled into the house in a daze again.

My mother's sister, Aunt Essie, was the only one home because my mother was at work. My cousin J.P., who gave me the car, and my brother were at work and I didn't want to disturb them. My aunt Essie never had children and so she was always the second mother in my life. I love Tyler Perry's version of Madea because my aunt Essie was the Madea in my life. She was big and tall and she dressed, talked, and walked like Madea. She always had a gun in her pocketbook during the day and under her pillow at night, but she never flashed it. Only close family members knew she had it. She always said that she would use it if she or her family felt threatened. My mother and their brother, Uncle Lannie, loved to tell stories about what a sharp shooter she was when they lived down South. They had to hunt and fish for their food. She never hurt anyone, but it was always our prayer that no one would ever make the mistake of crossing her.

So, as soon as I called and told her my situation, I was sorry, but she stayed calm. She said "you don't have to worry about your neighbors or worry about a car. What time does your next class start?" I told her it started at 11:00 a.m. and it was 7:00 a.m. at the time.

My father had died ten years earlier. My mother's brother, Lannie, had always been my father number two. About one hour after my call to my aunt, my mother and my uncle were at my door. They said, "Come on we are going to buy you a new car." My mother was glad because she didn't want me riding in that old car, anyway.

My mother's car was only three years old, so I insisted on my mother keeping the new car for herself and I took her car. I started crying because I couldn't afford the insurance. She said it would be cheaper to put it on her insurance because two cars and her age would give her a discount.

When we returned about 10:15 a.m. they told me to hurry up and I would make it to my next class on time. They went in my house as I left, pretending they had to go to the bathroom.

They sat by the window. I don't know how long and waited until the husband and wife came out of their house, then they went across the street and confronted my neighbors. I wonder if the fact that these two old people had the nerve to confront them reduced them to submission. Mom and Lannie told me later about their confrontation, but they said they were very quiet and respectful.

My Uncle Lannie told them that I would never do anything like go with her husband. He said that her husband was telling her the truth when he said he didn't even know my name. "So, I want you to know that we just bought her a new car and if anything ever happens to this one, the two of you will be found floating in the Delaware River, but no one will ever be able to find out how you got there." She said, "They didn't know anything about my windows being broken out." My uncle told them, "Well, do me a favor and pass the word through the neighborhood that if anything ever happens to her car again, the two of you will be held accountable and you'll be the one who will pay the price. So just pretend my niece is not over there."

REMEMBER THIS:

As a single parent raising your children without their father or mother to provide, protect and guide them. Everyone who loves you will find their own place in your life, but you have to be a friend to have a friend.

Hurting:

My separation hurt my mother and mother-in-law more than it hurt me. After I got past the hurt, shock, and devastation of my marriage crumbling, I didn't have time for self-pity. But my parents were on the outside looking in and watching my struggle and the poverty I lived in, and it hurt them deeply.

My mother-in-law moved to Albany, Georgia when she left Philadelphia, in 1972, and so she put $500 in a bank account and gave me the checkbook. She told me that if I ever had an emergency and needed money immediately, to take it out of this account. When she came home for my graduation from the University of Pennsylvania School of Social Work Master's Program, in 1989 I gave her the check book back with $500 in it. I thanked her and God that I never had an emergency serious enough to use that money.

CHAPTER 12

I GOT A NEW DAD

When my son Damon was ten years old and my daughter Kenya was seven years old, my mother-in-law Dorothy remarried. When he asked her to marry him, she explained that she had two grandchildren that her son had left and refused to pay her daughter-in-law child support. She told him that I never asked or admitted that I needed anything, she was always looking for ways to help me without offending me. She wanted him to know that she was going to do whatever she could think of to help me, and if he was going to have a problem with it, he shouldn't marry her, because she would not allow anyone to tell her what she could or could not do for us.

My new father-in-law's name was Albert and he stepped in as a natural father to me, and a grandfather to my children. He never had children, but he knew how to love us. And that's the main key to being a parent just knowing how to love people.

They were married for seventeen years. He took a large cardboard box and placed it in the kitchen. He would look for non-perishable items to send me. During that time, I never bought toilet paper, sugar, soap, or anything that you can think of that would not perish. When the box got full, they would send that one and start on a new box.

As I said before, they would just sit back and watch everything going on in my life. When the 1973 Chevy car that my mother gave me died in 1986, they bought themselves a new car and gave me their 1983 Ford Taurus. One of their neighbors in Albany, Georgia was coming to Philadelphia, so he drove it up here for them. A white man rung my bell and said, "I have a car outside for you. Your in-laws sent it to you." I had the money for my car insurance by that time.

My mother-in-laws' brothers, sisters, and cousins found their own ways of helping me, too. When they would have their family reunion, my in-laws would drive from Albany, Georgia to pick me and my children up. Her brother, Uncle Lawrence, would pay our hotel bill. Uncle Joe and Aunt Gladys would treat us to breakfast in the hotel, and my ex-husband's first cousins would treat my children to souvenirs and tours.

The older relatives were angry and disappointed in my ex-husband, but the first cousins kept their doors open to him. They have now reunited. As I said about first cousins, I think they knew some family secrets that I didn't know. This may be the reason they weren't as angry as their parents. They knew how to stay neutral and love and support me too.

When my mother-in-law died after seventeen years of marriage to my father-in-law, he moved to Philadelphia with me and he lived with me for seventeen years. I laugh about it now because I said when she married him I didn't know he would end up living with me for the same length of time that he lived with her.

My mother-in-law died of a sudden heart attack. When my ex-husband came to his mother's funeral, it was the first time he had seen her in twenty years.

One amazing thing happened at the repast after the funeral. I held the repast at Dorothy's sister Ella's house. My ex-husband went upstairs, he noticed that Aunt Ella still had our wedding picture hanging on her wall. He called me upstairs. He said, "Mary, all seven of your bridesmaids who were in our wedding are sitting downstairs." He couldn't even remember the names of the ushers on his side in the picture. I named them for him because I still had a relationship with most of them too. My in-law's family loved me and I became the caregiver for Albert and Dorothy's sister Ella for a while.

CHAPTER 13

BODY LANGUAGE

I knew when my husband left me that something was seriously wrong with him emotionally , however, he would never tell me the truth about what it was. I also knew that if I didn't let him see the children when he would show up, they would put all types of information in their mind to fill the void, and probably blame themselves.

Once when my son was nine years old, I put him on the Trailway bus to visit his Dad in Baltimore. (I would never do that in the present day.) When I went to pick him up from the Trailway Bus Station, I could see my son sitting in the lobby through the glass doors. I could tell from his posture that something was wrong. I couldn't get through those double doors fast enough. I asked him "What happened to you in Baltimore?" He said, "Nothing." All the way home he kept saying "nothing." I sat him in a chair and stared in his eyes and I told him that he could not move away from my stare until he told me what happened to him in Baltimore. Finally, he said, "Daddy cried the whole time I was there, especially after he put me on the bus." I got on the phone and called him. I told him that I knew that something happened to my son in Baltimore and I wanted him to tell me what happened because Damon would not tell me (I wanted to see if their stories matched). He said, "I just couldn't stop crying because I miss my family so much."

I told him that he should talk to a friend or go to counseling to help him adjust, because he couldn't upset his son like that again. He said, "Okay." I told Damon that we would wait until he was a little older before he went away for a weekend with his Dad again. I told his Dad to come on weekends to Philadelphia, to plan some fun activities with one of his friends that Damon knew. But to just keep him and his daughter, Kenya out a day at a time while visiting them. He said, "Okay." He did it one time and it went well.

But the next summer he asked for both of them together. Kenya was seven and Damon was ten years old. He said that he made plans with his friends in Baltimore who had children their age.

They arrived on a Friday evening. Kenya called me on Saturday morning at 6:00 a.m. She said she could hear her father crying all night long in the next room. She stayed awake all night long and every time her brother Damon would fall asleep she would hit him until he would wake up and sit up with her. Kenya, at seven years old, told her brother that she was afraid to go to sleep because sometimes when people are that upset they will kill their family and themselves. As soon as the sun came up, she called me. She said, "I want to come home right now because Daddy can't stop crying." I told him to put them on the next train running. He said he didn't know they heard him, but he had bought tickets to the circus and his friends were going to take their children. I said, "No, they are not comfortable, send them home now." When they got off the train I asked Damon if he was scared because he had witnessed it before. He said Kenya talked all night long, so he began to believe he should have been scared before and now. He said he felt sorry for his Dad and he knew that he needed help, but he didn't want to go back.

So, their Dad would come about once a year and spend a day or two with them in Philadelphia, but four years later he asked them to come to Baltimore for a weekend again. When they arrived, their father was moving into a new rented house. He said that he rented it for us because he wanted me to move to Baltimore with them. He said he was going to keep Damon because he is becoming a young man now, and needed him to launch him into manhood. I said, "Well, you left me saying you were going to the store and never came back. I would be afraid to send you to the store for bread. Why would I move in a rented house with you when you walked off and left me in a house you bought for me? You have not sent me a dime for child support since you left, so I consider you too fragile to ever lean on again."

"Plus, Damon needed you just as much at age five when he started kindergarten as he does now." He could not concentrate or perform in kindergarten or first grade. He left the week Damon started kindergarten in school. He couldn't figure out where his father was or what happened to him. He was restless and unable to perform all the way through school. The teachers recommended that he be put on Ritalin. I'm glad I didn't because I now know that there are serious side effects to the long-term use of Ritalin.

Because I wouldn't agree to move to Baltimore, he tried to talk Damon into it, saying he wanted to live with him. He was planning to take me to court for custody if Damon wanted to come. Damon kept saying "It doesn't matter what we say, Mommy's not going to let it happen." He told Damon to go home and get his things packed and he would come for him the next weekend, that he would handle me himself because he thought he could come with a court order.

Well, when he called to see if Damon was ready Damon said, "Mommy and Kenya need me. I'm not going to run off and leave them alone." (Like you did.) That was the end of that conversation.

CHAPTER 14

RITALIN: KIDDIE CRACK

I worked as a medical social worker for Jefferson Hospital's Rebound Children and Youth Medical Center in Philadelphia. I was a social worker for foster care and adoption and I spent the last twenty years of my career as a social worker for homeless families and individuals.

I have had the experience of talking to many parents, teenagers, and small children. In all of my positions I have worked as a child advocate for parents and children between the school and medical systems. Reviewing IEPs (Individual Educational Plans) for children who have physical disabilities, who were in foster care or up for adoption or living in shelters for the homeless. I taught parents how to read report cards and their child's IEP plan. I learned myself that the grade "A" did not mean an "A" at the top of their class. You had to know at what level your child was on, at an "A" level. For example: your child could be reading on level three in 3rd grade and receiving an "A" grade for level 3 not level 1. Level 1 was the correct level for their grade.

Many teenagers have told me that their abuse with prescription drugs started in elementary school when they were prescribed Ritalin or other mood altering drugs. Of course, if it is used as prescribed it may never lead to serious damage to their kidneys or other organs. However, many students and parents have told me that by the time the children reach teenagers they have learned and believe that you can and should alter your moods with prescription or street drugs. You look for whatever makes you feel good at the moment.

That's why I call Ritalin and other mood altering drugs, Kiddie Crack.

Because of my experience with my son, I could identify with the difficulty that many parents had with the school and medical systems when looking for the proper help for their child. They have various special needs, but do not necessarily need prescription drugs.

In the early 1970s, funding became available for special needs children under Title 20. Many, many black children, especially black boys, were diagnosed as ADHD (Attention Deficit Hyperactivity Disorder), because this label would give the schools extra funding. Because these children were black and some were poor it was assumed that their behavior was dysfunctional.

Where is Daddy?

In 1973, my son was seven years old and in the second grade at a Catholic school. My husband left the week my son started kindergarten. I saw the change in him immediately. He was unable to focus or concentrate in school. Teachers said that they would have to call on him several times to get his attention. He was confused and deeply hurt. Where had his loving, devoted father gone? He couldn't understand. I told him that his daddy and I weren't getting along anymore so daddy and I separated. But what did that have to do with him? Daddy wasn't calling or coming around. What did "we're not getting along" mean? We were not arguing or fighting in front of him. Suddenly, Daddy was just gone. I couldn't tell him that Daddy had an emotional breakdown. So, I explained it the best way that I could.

One day, the principal of the Catholic school, which he attended, called me. She said Damon picked a chair up and threatened to hit a teacher with it. I got so upset, I assumed that he had just broken down emotionally because he was upset about his Daddy leaving. She told me that she called a school psychologist to meet with us the next day. I said okay. When I arrived at the school the next day, the psychologist was waiting outside on the steps for us.

He was a skinny white man. He had on white striped pants above his ankles and his hair was standing straight up on his head like a punk rocker. He had worn run over shoes and no coat. This was February 1973. I knew that I would not respect or trust his opinion on anything. I never got out of the car. I drove straight to Children's Hospital of Philadelphia to the Child Guidance Center. They assigned us to Dr. Clifford Bell, a black male psychologist. I told him that I thought my son was having an emotional breakdown because he was so upset about losing his father. The principal told me on the phone the previous day that Damon needed psychiatric help and needed to be put on Ritalin because he had ADHD and serious behavioral problems. Dr. Bell took Damon into his office alone, when he called me in he said, "Did you ever ask your son what happened?" He told Damon to tell me.

Damon said "The teacher called on me to read and I didn't know where to start. She told me to go into the coat closet." I said "No" and so she snatched me out of my chair and tried to put me in the closet. I picked up a chair and told her I would hit her with the chair if she tried again to put me in the closet. She called the principal to come and she took me to the office."

Dr. Bell said, mother, let us applaud your son. He handled that situation appropriately. He said that he would go to the school and meet with the principal and the teacher. He would let them know that they did not handle the situation appropriately. His previous teachers acknowledged that he had problems concentrating, but he was not ADHD. They showed patience and would help him reconnect so he could focus on the class assignment. All of his teachers noted how intelligent he was until he went to 2ⁿᵈ grade.

Dr. Bell also told them that he agreed with me and that my son would not be put on Ritalin. The principal said the only other child she saw who was as violent as Damon was institutionalized. He told them that he would meet with my son weekly for 5 months until the end of June, and he would monitor his behavior and theirs closely. He would help him with his homework to increase his classroom participation because Damon was very intelligent. He told them he did not anticipate Damon having any problem with his class work.

I had another incident with them because Damon took an apple in the bathroom. He had an apple in his hand and he had to go to the bathroom, but he didn't know what to do with the apple, so he took it with him and laid it on the sink. They degraded him by calling him nasty and giving him some ridiculous punishment. I squashed that punishment.

Dr. Bell did not want me to take Damon out of the school. He said "Let him stay until the end of the term and start fresh in a new school in September. Sometimes it's better to let them stay in a situation until the appropriate time to move them. Let them work on and around the situation in their own way. Damon knows that he has our support and we will be listening to him."

Dr. Bell brought me in for a couple sessions of therapy. He let me know that I was so hurt and disappointed about my husband leaving that I was letting my guilt cloud my judgment. I assumed that everything that was happening to Damon was a result of his pain from his father leaving. That incident did not have anything to do with his father leaving.

When professionals feed into the stereotypes that they are taught about children who are black and they assume are poor and underprivileged, plus they are angry and dissatisfied with their own life, they take their frustration out on the children under their care. We could call it institutional racism.

I never asked my son what happened. I missed the opportunity to deal with it the first day she called. But it all worked out because Damon and I both benefitted from the short-term counseling with Dr. Bell. That's when I learned that we cannot fill the void when our children feels the loss of a love one. We cannot fix them. We can only provide a quiet, loving, supportive home for them where they can grow and adapt to the change. They have to develop their own strategies and mechanisms for coping with loss and disappointments.

Dr. Bell said, "Don't you kill his spirit or let anyone else kill his spirit by putting him in a closet or putting him on drugs."

I took Damon to dinner that weekend to celebrate his spirit and to let him know I was proud of him. I apologized to him. He let his teacher know that she could not do that to him. I told him that we sometimes have to teach people how to treat us and let them know what we will not accept.

That's confidence and he had plenty of that.

I said in my introduction that I could see how my setbacks were my set ups for my comeback. Because of this experience and what I learned in counseling from Dr. Bell, I felt confident when working with doctors, school systems, parents, and children as an advocate for children and parents' rights.

CHAPTER 15

INSTITUTIONAL RACISM

I nstitutional racism, classism, crime, and lack of spiritualism permeates our whole society.

Instutional Racism:

When one nationality degrades, demoralizes, colonizes, enslaves, or limits the growth of another race or nation because of their race or religion, or just because they have the power and the resources to do so, to create a lower class or eradicate a nationality.

Classism:

When one group of people places others in a caste system in their minds because they have the resources and power to do so. Black and white people are guilty of classism. Anytime politicians, the board of education, and the criminal justice system develop policies based solely on a persons economic status, it is classism.

It's The Haves vs. The Have Nots:

I have recently heard of a case where black teachers of special education students in kindergarten mistreat and abuse five year olds. They believe that these children's biggest problems are a lack of discipline and they need to be whipped into shape. They are treating these students the same way in 2014 that my son was treated in 1973. The teacher that witnessed it reported what she had seen. She is waiting to see if authorities are going to address the issue.

I have seen black policemen stop and search the car of another young black man because he was driving an expensive car. They assumed he was a drug dealer. In one incident that I witnessed, the police snatched the young man out of his car and made him spread eagle on the hood of his car. His wife walked up and showed her I.D.; she was a civil rights lawyer. I don't know what happened, but I hope she pursued a case against those officers.

I know friends of mine whose children have grown up, became very successful, moved to the suburbs and will not come back to their old neighborhood to visit their parents. All of the above is classism.

Spiritualism:

Crime is sometimes due to a lack of spiritualism—criminals have no moral compass. When one person or system commits a crime against others, it takes us all into a downward spiral. Especially when it comes to black on black crime, but all nationalities have a destructive component within their on village. It does not make sense and I can only attribute it to the lack of spiritualism. I don't believe that one person can hurt another person or take someone else's life if they love themselves or know God. Unless they are mentally ill.

CHAPTER 16

LABELS: AGAINST ALL ODDS

Labels: Published by the Philadelphia Daily News, Monday, January 27, 1986.
Label a child too stupid to learn and you have a Thomas Edison.

Label a man a hopeless alcoholic and you have a Bill Wilson, founder of Alcoholics Anonymous.

Label a man so seriously mentally ill that he cuts off his own ear and you have a Vincent Van Gogh.

Label a man dull and hopeless and flunk him in the sixth grade and you have a President, Winston Churchill.

Label a boy who cared more about drawing than homework and you have a Walt Disney.

Label a person blind and unable to see and you have a Ray Charles, George Shearing, Stevie Wonder, and Tom Sullivan.

Label a man paralytic and you have a British fighter pilot who lost both legs in an air crash, fly again with the RAF and you have Douglas Bader, who, with two artificial limbs, was captured by the Germans three times during World War II and escaped three times.

Label a child at birth, deaf, blind, and mute and you have a Helen Keller

Now:

Label a child born with no hands and a club foot and you have my godson Sian Williams, an MBA Accountant for the Federal Government.

Label a child disabled who lost his sight when he was young and you have Dr. Andre Watson, a psychiatrist at Jefferson Hospital in Philadelphia.

Label a child abused, neglected or homeless and considered disadvantaged and you have Oprah Winfrey, Tyler Perry, and Tavis Smiley.

Label a child 7 years old as violent and you have my son Damon Halliday, Pastor of a Church, and one of the most humble, compassionate human being that can be found.

Label the child of a single working class mother with limited resources as disadvantaged and you have the first black President of the United States, Barack Obama.

And I think that it is not, despite all of the odds that the above persons became successful, but because of all the obstacles they faced, they gained the strength to overcome.

I like the song that "God specializes and He can do what no other power, but the Holy Ghost Power can do."

CHAPTER 17

SCHOOL DROPOUT

Well, Damon never did anything in school. He would usually take test so he could pass to the next grade. But in the eleventh grade, he received all F's on his 1st report period. When I went to parent's night and the teacher gave me his report card, I was shocked. I asked the teacher, "How can someone get all F's?" She said, "Because he does not come to school." I asked him "Why didn't you tell me you weren't going to school?" He said, "You didn't ask me if I was going to school." I was really struggling at that time to come up with lunch money and tokens, plus clothes and sneakers. Sneakers were very important to him. He needed a pair for style along with basketball, baseball, and track. I had received my bachelor's degree, but I wasn't making much money.

I went home and just went to bed. He couldn't believe I didn't fuss. He kept saying "I'm going to do better." I knew what that meant. He would bring his grades up to D's by his fourth report period. That was no longer acceptable.

I woke up at 6:00 a.m. in the morning with my answer, clear as a bell. I was going to do what I had always feared would happen; he would drop out of school. I woke him up and told him to gather his books. He was going to turn them in and quit school. The teachers, coaches, and principal came running. They begged me not to take him out of school. I told them that I would never again give him a dime for lunch, carfare, or clothes. On the way home, I said, "You already have one job washing dishes. So, get two more dishwashing jobs. You need one job for your spending money, one job to pay me rent, and one job for savings, so you'll have some money when you are ready to move.

But if I ever find out you are doing anything illegal you will be put out immediately with no notice." He called his father, who came to get him. I said, "You are not going anywhere. You will stay here until we can work this out together. I do not want you to think that I do not love you or I'm throwing you away."

Well, he laid in his bed depressed for weeks. He said he was afraid to go outside because our neighbors would see him and ask why he wasn't in school. I said, "You weren't going to school anyway." I didn't know until later that our neighbor Ms. Brenda had called him. She let him know that she had heard about him dropping out of school. She told him that she was very disappointed in him because she had always considered him a role model for her two young sons.

He woke up one morning and he said, "I'm going to commit suicide because you ruined my life." I said, "Fine, if that's the way you decide to handle your problems. You have three solutions to your problems: stay depressed, use drugs, or commit suicide. But you could also get a general education diploma and you can get a job and go to college on a GED." I told him to go to the library, and get the information. When I came home from work the next day he had registered for his classes. He said he was going to take five classes because there were five parts to the test.

I told him, "You are smarter than you know you are. Take the test and see which tests you can pass. Then you can concentrate on the courses you need." He said, "Okay." I had just started a new job. I was sitting at my desk on the second floor. I could hear someone screaming Mommy, Mommy! He ran into my office and said, "I busted that GED test wide open. I do not have to take any classes."

I said, "Fine. Now you can look for a better job and if you ever decide to go to college, you can." A couple weeks later a marketing firm called and asked for him. I said "He isn't home. Can I take a message?" The caller said that he applied for a job at their marketing firm and to tell him to report to work at 9 a.m. tomorrow morning.

He was playing basketball in the schoolyard up the street, two blocks away. I ran all the way. He saw me coming and ran to meet me. I told him he got the job. The next morning, he put on his three-piece suit, a long navy blue overcoat, and picked up one of his fathers' briefcases. He went outside with his friends who were on the corner waiting for the trolley with their book bags. They asked him, "Where are you going with a briefcase?" He said, "To work." Well, it turned out that the owner of the firm, Mr. Morris Davis, lived on our block. My son had never noticed him, but he had watched my son playing basketball and interacting with others on the block. He took my son under his wing and taught him the business at the age of sixteen.

Girls need their father's too:

My daughter Kenya still reminds me that losing her father at the age of two years old created a great void in her life. I never worried about my daughter and the important decisions I made for her. I thought we were very close after the age of sixteen. I thought that I understood her and her needs because I was a female and I had plenty of girlfriends to talk to about the stages of her development. But she still tells me that I really didn't understand because I grew up with my father.

My father was very serious about providing and protecting his family. He left most issues regarding family and home up to my mother, until he felt that one of those issues were at risk. Then you saw the other side of him; he became the hulk. He was like Iyanla and Tyler Perry said, "He was a father to my brother and a Daddy to me."

My daughter did not have that and she said she missed it. She had plenty of uncles and cousins who adored her and were very close to her. But she still says, "That's not the same."

This is how I know that you cannot take away your children's pain or fix everything for them in their life. They have to grow, adapt, and process their own personal experiences. No one knows how another person feels regarding loss or disappointments. All we can do is love our children and give them whatever it is we have to give, and accept the fact that you cannot be their mother and father.

She was very angry and rebellious from the ages of thirteen to fifteen, but it seems that she changed on her sixteenth birthday. I praised the Lord because she became much more compliant and willing to please. She still had issues that I knew were a result of her father not being in her life. So I sought answers to help us with this issue. I wanted her to have the opinion of a man who was Christ-centered and so we started going to Rev. Floyd's school. Rev. Floyd was an ex-policeman who had worked in gang control in the 60s, just as my ex-husband did when I married him in 1963.

My husband was a plainclothes detective in gang control, but they didn't know each other. That job weighed heavy on my husband as it did on Rev. Floyd. They both told me stories of going to families to take them to the morgue to identify their sons killed in gang warfare. This was devastating to both of them. Both of them had to quit their jobs. My husband never found another decent paying job and he sank into a deep depression, eventually he just left everybody I thought he loved. I asked him to come back home, so we could go to counseling together, but he would not do it. He did the worst thing that a person can do when they are depressed he isolated himself.

This experience in the police department motivated Rev. Floyd to buy a van and put a casket on top. He wanted to keep the community confronted with the issues of gang violence. He would take gang members to the morgue to see what they were doing to each other and what could happen to them. He would also take gang members to prison to talk to old prison inmates who had life sentences.

CHAPTER 18

CHRONOLOGICAL AGE VS. DEVELOPMENTAL AGE

R ev. Floyd says, "The biggest problem with crime is on the family breakdown. The main problem is single parents raising their sons and daughters alone."

His topic that night: Tootsie and T-Bone started going together at the age of eighteen and became sexually active and became parents. Tootsie, developmentally, is only sixteen years old, and T-Bone is only fourteen years old developmentally.

Of course, he wants to get married to his girlfriend, the love of his life. After all, he had a good job as a stock boy in a department store. But she wanted him to bring home his whole pay check to pay rent, utilities, food, diapers, and clothes for her and the baby.

Well, since there was no way his paycheck could cover all those things, he might as well buy himself a new pair of sneakers and a sweat shirt. After all, he was the one going out to work. Well, now most of his check is gone. He knows she's going to be mad because she was mad when he left that morning. He didn't get up in time to put the trash out, for the third week in a row. She wasn't going to get up to do it or wake him up in time to do it because that was his job. It was her job to take care of the baby, and not much else.

So, the smart thing to do was to stop on the corner with the boys and play a card game, called three hand molly or shoot some dice. Oh my! He wasn't so lucky. So, he and the boys would go into the beer garden to get some beer and sit down and wait until she went to sleep. But guess what? She and the baby went to her mother's house because they were hungry. Now she is angry with him and so is her mother. Mother just does not understand why this man, who is fourteen years old developmentally, is not a responsible husband.

Now Tootsie is going to tell her daughter that she does not have to get married just because she is pregnant. T-Bone will tell his son and other young boys that they do not have to get married just because a girl is pregnant. Buy the baby some milk and diapers, and when he starts walking, buy him some shoes. Take him to the movies every now and then with his current girlfriend's children or his other children, so they will know each other. At least he's being involved and responsible for some things, he thinks.

This is how dysfunction is passed on to the next generation. This new generation of children can't even give you their last name (they only know their nickname) or first name. They don't know their parents last names and addresses at the age of five years old because they have already moved five times in five years. Mom and Dad have sometimes changed partners three times each. This is information that we had to know before we started kindergarten.

I was a social work supervisor in the Intake Department for the Office of Shelter and Services for the Homeless in the mid 80's. There were approximately 2,500 mothers with children in homeless shelters and approximately 2,500 single men and women in shelters, also. These statistics were the current numbers when I was in graduate school for a master's in social work in 1987.

Well, back to Rev. Floyd's story about T-Bone and Tootsie. Rev. Floyd would act out this whole story and he was an excellent comic. He talked to the teenagers about having short and long-term goals for themselves. "Map out a plan for your life and know what steps you have to take on a daily basis to reach your goals. Also, know what type of girlfriends and boyfriends you have to invite into your circle to reach your goals. Talk to each other, iron sharpens iron and minds sharpen minds."

Well, because he was so funny in telling this story, my daughter was on the floor laughing by the time he finished talking. She went up and shook his hand and told him that she will have dinner ready every Thursday so we would be on time and she did. He had 120 topics dated and she knew exactly what he would be talking about at each session. She circled the topics she was most interested in and invited her friends to join her.

One of the things that fascinated her the most is that the elderly men and women took notes and she wanted to know why. I told her that they were still examining their own lives and figuring out what to tell their children and grandchildren. None of us want them to make the mistakes that we made. Every generation wants more for the next generation and community.

CHAPTER 19

INDEPENDENCE

My daughter decided to attend Shaw University in Raleigh, North Carolina, when she graduated from high school. My son, who gained confidence in himself from working, decided to quit his job and go with her.

When my children left for college, I wasn't worried about my daughter. I knew she was well grounded in the Word of God and armed with 120 of Melvin Floyd's tapes. She would play his tapes every Sunday for her girlfriends.

My son told me he was sick of me and the church and he was not going to church ever again after the age of eighteen. So, at the age of eighteen, he stopped. But when he moved to North Carolina, he found a church the first Sunday he was there. When I asked him about it he said, "I'm not crazy, I'm not going to be in a strange city with no friends or family. I knew that I needed a church family at least." He became a very committed active member in the church and made some lifetime friends of his own.

Look for the good:

I always knew my son Damon was smart and kind-hearted, so I tried not to let my concern about school overshadow my entire relationship with him.

It felt good when people from the outside would come to me and say good things about him, too.

His teacher spoke highly of him:

When Damon was in the fourth grade in Mitchell Elementary School, his teacher called one night. Her name was also Mrs. Mitchell. She said that she mentioned that she was Jewish. She said that Damon stayed in for recess to talk to her. He tried to convert her from Judaism to Christianity.

She said that he did not convert her, but he presented a pretty persuasive arguement. She said that she had not met me yet because school had just started, but she was looking forward to meeting me. She said that I was doing an excellent job of raising my son because he was a very kind, polite, and thoughtful child.

Our neighbors spoke highly of him:
    One night after Damon left for college, my neighbors rang my bell and asked for Damon. It was Mr. Hudson, our committee man, and Mr. Grooms, our block captain. They said that Mr. Hudson was going to retire soon as our committee man, and Mr. Grooms would move into his position. They wanted to take Damon under their wing and prepare him to become the next block captain, and eventually the committeeman. They said the block committee had all agreed that Damon was the best candidate because he had the respect of the young and old residents on our block.

My heart soared because I always knew that he was a good guy.
    My Pastor Rev. Dr. M. Peace predicted that my son would preach one day. There was a young man in our church named Scott Mann. He was very close to my son Damon. His mother Yvonne was one of my best friends. Scott was a lifeguard for the city. In 1980, Scott drowned as a lifeguard in a city pool. Scott was very active with the Baptist Congress of Christian Education. They dedicated their next speaker's contest to Scott. They also initiated a scholarship to children who were active in the Congress in Scott Mann's name. Children from churches all over the city would compete in the speaker's contest.
    Damon who said he couldn't read in front of people agreed to represent our church in Scott's name in the contest. Damon did not win the contest, but when he finished speaking my pastor Rev. Dr. Marquette Peace turned to me and said, "Damon will preach one day." I said, "I can't even get the boy to go to school." He said, "I don't care, one day he will preach."

Marijuana:
    I was still worried about my son when he was leaving home because I knew he liked to smoke marijuana. I prayed that he would give it up and not move on to cocaine. What I didn't know was that a girl on the block who had inherited a lot of money introduced some of the kids to cocaine. My son said that she came into the room when they were all high and laid cocaine on the table and everyone in the room took a hit—except for my son. He said that he was high already, but when it came his turn, he said, "No, thank you." When he got home, he fell on the floor and thanked God that he had not taken a hit with everyone else.
    He promised God that he would never be tempted with anything else again, because he would never allow anything else to pass his lips again: not a cigarette, marijuana, or an alcohol beverage. That's when he made the decision to go to college with his sister and get out of the neighborhood. Like we used to say in my day, "God, if you get me out of this situation, I won't come back."

Now, when he looks back and wonders why he walked away that night, he remembers the times he was leaving the house at night and his mother would be on her knees praying at her bedside.

I didn't know about his experience until he came home to preach at his friend's funeral. He said, "I was with him the night he took his first hit." He preached on the "Prodigal Son." He said, "if you are on the wrong track, come back home to your family and friends, they are waiting for you with open arms. It's never too late." Many of the children who grew up on the block with him were at the funeral. About six of them accepted Christ at the funeral.

Pray without ceasing:

I still stay on my knees praying for myself and my children because we're never too old to be beyond temptation. That's why Jesus tells us how to pray in Matthew 6:9. We are to pray "Our Father who art in heaven, hallowed be thy name. Thy kingdom come, thy will be done on earth, as it is in heaven." In Matthew 6:13, he says, "Lead us not into temptation, but deliver us from evil." We should use this prayer every night, because a new temptation that we never experienced before may confront us in the morning.

CHAPTER 20

LETTER FROM MOTHER TO SON

I did not know about his experiences with drugs when he was leaving for school. I decided to write the following letter to him in his Bible.

Dear Son,

Please keep this Bible and apply it as life moves along.

Find a church that teaches the Bible because an understanding of God our Creator will carry you further than any Bachelor degree.

Remember, God wants our obedience, attention, glory, honor, and acknowledgment of His power.

Obedience—by knowing and living His word.

Attention—He is going to get that, but give it to Him first in prayer.

Glory and Honor—Go to His house of worship and join others in His promise.

Power—Acknowledge that He not only has power over our death but over our everyday life too.

If we're obedient to God, He'll shower us with blessings, too numerous to count.

Mommy

September 5, 1986

CHAPTER 21

I COULDN'T PRAY

I have always told my children to stay close to God and to hold onto his unchanging hand because you can be hit with a tragedy that you didn't see coming. So, if you don't already know God for yourself, you won't have time to go find him. God has to already be carrying you.

Now, I know that's what was happening to me when my mother got sick.

My mother was sick with cirrhosis of the liver, from Hepatitis C. Now, we've only known this to come from alcohol abuse. The doctors said that's what caused it, but my mother never drank or smoked anything. When I told her sister and brother her diagnosis they said "What? We're the one's who drank and smoked and she was the one who got cirrhosis."

My Uncle Lannie went to talk to her doctor. This was good because he knew her medical history better than my brother Milton or I did. It turns out that she had two major operations in the 1940s. Her doctor said that blood could not be screened or cleaned thoroughly during that time and so that's when she probably contracted Hepatitis C and yes it took fifty years to kill her. It was hard to believe but true.

Well, that's a horrible death to witness, when I would visit her I would just be in awe. I was shocked at the huge changes that her body could go through in one day. Sometimes she would be green in the morning and look like an inflated balloon by evening. Her eyes had rolled back in her head and she laid unconscious for six weeks.

I couldn't pray. It felt like my tongue was tied. I asked God to take her, but after her death I walked around in a daze because I was still in shock from what I'd seen. She died a horrible death. Why God? She ate healthy and lived a clean and sober life.

It was hard to understand or accept, but I finally made peace with it. Because she was unconscious I had to believe she was not in pain or aware of her suffering. Her old body was just slowly shutting down, but she had already won her crown and gone to glory.

CHAPTER 22

SICK: BUT NOT UNTO DEATH

I got sick in November 1997. I woke up with a blinding headache. When I went into the hospital I could not sit up, open my eyes, or move my head. I stayed five days and they sent me home because they said that all the tests were negative. They said that I was just having migraine headaches and a lot of people live with migraines and go to work. So, they would not give me a letter for a leave of absence from work.

Well, I couldn't go to work because I couldn't sit up or open my eyes. They told me not to come back to the emergency room because I had already been given all of the tests and they couldn't find anything wrong with me. Well, one day when I begged to go back into the hospital they referred me to Dr. Patricia Ford, a hematologist. I went to see Dr. Ford on Christmas Eve. When I walked into her office she said "you have a rare blood disease called cold agglutinin hemolytic anemia." Antibodies are eating up your red blood cells. "You have a headache because you are not getting enough oxygen to your brain."

She had everything ready for a blood transfusion. After I had been on the machine for about four hours she came into the room and asked if I still had a headache. I said "No." My transfusions take eight hours all together. She said that my disease is related to Leukemia. I don't have cancer of the blood, but my disease is incurable. She told me to come back every two weeks for a follow-up. Well, I went back every two weeks and each time I needed a transfusion. I asked what will happen when my blood does not last two weeks?

Dr. Ford said, "You can't live long like this. You may only live two or three months like this." I wasn't on any medication because they did not have a cure for this disease.

However, whenever I would have a transfusion I would feel fine for two weeks and I lost very little time from work.

Well this went on for two years and I didn't die. Then Dr. Ford said she wanted to put me on a medicine that she uses for leukemia patients. She originally thought it would be too strong for me. I said, "Yes, I'll try it."

That's when I started on Procrit. It's been like a miracle drug to me. I go into crisis and I've had fifty-four blood transfusions in 18 years, but I'm still here. Basically, it stabilizes me. I am fine on a daily basis. I'm able to travel, baby sit my great grandchildren and live a fairly active life. Surprisingly, I didn't get scared or upset when she said I only had months to live. I accepted this prognosis. I got busy putting my business in order. I never cried or asked God why me? I just felt that God was carrying me along the path he laid for me and I accepted his will.

Transferred Grief:

I thought I was alright and taking it well, until I would think about my Aunt Essie. I was her baby. I kept imagining the expression that would be on her face when my children tell her that I have died. Whenever I would think about leaving her I would collapse in tears.

My son asked why I was crying for my Aunt, "What about Kenya and I?" I said, "The two of you will have to get over my death because you have children to raise." I am so special to my Aunt, I don't know who will look after her, after I'm gone.

She had my brother Milton and my cousin Delores, but Delores lived out of town and my brother worked out of town. I went to see her everyday and she knew that there was nothing that I wouldn't do for her. I was her baby, her life line, she thought.

My son came from Dallas, Texas to talk to my doctor, so he could understand what care I might need. The doctor couldn't really say what my end would be like or how debilitating it would be.

But, one of the main characteristics of the disease was, I could not go outside in the winter. After a few weeks she said I could return to work if I rode in a heated car. So, my brother took me to work and picked me up for months, going into his job late and leaving early to accommodate me.

Angel In Disguise:

Then, guess what? A young lady who worked with me for years but we weren't friends, asked for me. When my friend at work told her my situation, that because of my chronic anemia I could not come outside in extreme cold weather. She said, "I live near her, I'll pick her up and take her home everyday." She called me and said, "My car will be nice and warm by the time I get to your house." I said, "OK."

She not only drove me back and forth to work, she would go out to get my lunch every day, and if I said that I didn't have any money because I had not been able to get to the bank, she would lend me money.

So, after about two months my son told me to tell her just how much he appreciated her. He called her, "Our angel." The next morning, I didn't know why I was so hype. I could hardly wait until she stopped her car. I got in and I told her that I thought God had put us together for a special reason.

She said she felt that way too. We started witnessing and testifying to each other. She told me that she had a bad heart and she had lost a brother and a sister to sudden heart attacks. She told me the story of her life and how she was not afraid to die because she knew God. I told her the same thing and that I accepted whatever is God's will for my life.

The next morning she said she was staying home because she had a cold. On the second day her husband called to tell me Darlene had died of a heart attack. I was shocked.

Message from Dr. Ford; my hematologist,

I have had the pleasure of caring for Mary Halliday for many years as she endured a rare blood disease—cold agglutinin hemolytic anemia. Her body destroys her red blood cells. This makes her very anemic leading to chronic exhaustion and life threatening anemic when she has the flu. She has lived with the disease and other infirmities with dignity, grace, and perseverance. I am sure she fights daily to live a normal life as possible with a positive attitude. On every office visit she is pleasant and upbeat. I admire her strength, her love of family and life and am sure she will continue as she always has living each day to its fullest.

Best,
Dr. Patricia Ford

Sick again: but covered by the blood.

I got sick twice in 2014. I had tumors in the right side of my thyroid that pushed my thyroid down into my chest. Then a mass of tumors formed around it in my chest. The doctors thought they were cancerous, but there was no cancer in any of the mass.

As I stated before, I've had 54 blood transfusions because of the rare blood disease for anemia.

I called my hematologist to ask her why I had not been scheduled for a blood transfusion before surgery, because my blood count never goes over 7.0, because of my disease.

Dr. Ford stated that my pre-operation blood test showed my hemoglobin at 9.7. It has never been 9.7. Especially, in the winter. She said the blood would be in the operating room when I needed it. I went in and out of surgery two times with out needing blood.

In January 2015, I had surgery on my knee and my blood count was still 9.4 Now, its summer and my count should have stayed up, but it has dropped to 7.4. God does what he wants to do, when he wants and how he wants to.

CHAPTER 23

DEVELOPING A REPROBATE MIND

When we turn against God's Word, He allows us to develop a reprobate mind. I learned that when we lower the values and standards that were set and practiced by our Christian ancestors we develop a reprobate mind. That's when wrong begins to look right and initially it feels good.

There are four ways of bringing dysfunction and chaos to ourselves, families, and our communities:

1.Spiritually:

Rejecting God's Word causes us to lose our spiritual vision and to accept the false doctrine of man.

2.Morally:

Surrendering to sensuality in our thinking, dress, and behavior, etc. This leads to the acceptance of immorality. It's now alright to be nude and have sex on film.

3.Mentally:

The wrong philosophical and psychological theories on life leads to stress and disappointment all in search of money, love, peace, fun, and success.

4.Physically:

A decline in the above areas leads to physical suicide through illness, drugs, alcohol abuse or actually committing murder or suicide.

Television, music, literature, and social media promote the following: fighting, disrespect to parents and teachers and violent gang attacks in schools and the community for fun. We had to close schools across the city for a day or two to cool down because the children were attacking each other and staff members. Yes we entertain ourselves with television and videos that show young people how to respond, interact and communicate violently. But when we, our children, or someone in our community is the victim, we ask why? Three thirteen year olds from different sections of Philadelphia planned and met each other on the Temple University campus and seriously injured several students using bricks as weapons.

What voices and values have they grown up listening to in their village to make them think this was a fun way to spend their evening?

CHAPTER 24

SHAME

Stop! Turn Your Mess Into A Message:

When 50 cent and other rappers were singing lyrics that were demeaning to women, calling them the b#### word and other degrading words, there was an outcry from ministers like Calvin Butts, politicians like C. Delores Tucker and many community leaders.

I was embarrassed and ashamed. I could not wrap my mind around a man or a woman looking at me and having a negative thought in their head about me.

I certainly didn't think it would be accepted by most women who were educated or came from homes with any integrity or values.

But now we have reality shows with women fighting, gossiping and calling each other the b#### word.

The musicians and actors say that they are just telling their story about life as they know it. Well I guess I can't argue with that point if that's been their experience. But don't allow those sad stories to permeate our entire culture. They do not represent all poor people. Our forefathers were poor but they had dignity and class.

Who's writing new stories about their experiences celebrating marriage, birth of a child, or our love for our family and friends in our village?

I worked as a social worker for the homeless and I have many stories of accomplishment and families overcoming what looked like insurmountable problems, but have stories of victory. They should be told.

How low have we fallen? What impact do our performers think these messages of degradation and violence will have on their children? Where do their children go from here?

Jeremiah 2:5, What fault did your father find in me, that they strayed so far from me? They followed worthless idols and became worthless themselves.

Jeremiah 2:9, I will bring charges against your children's' children.

I Corinthian 15:13, "Do not be misled: Bad company corrupts good character. Come back to your senses as you ought and stop sinning for there are some who are ignorant of God, I say this to your shame."

Remember this:

If you don't tell your children about Jesus, you will tell Jesus about your children.

CHAPTER 25

SIN

My Mama and my Papa would say, you better shop around for your friends Think seriously about all of the decisions you make.

Make sure you have your mad money on you when you leave home. Never leave your food or drink unattended. Don't turn your back on your food either. If you feel uncomfortable in a place, trust your instincts and leave.

They encouraged me to buy my own car at the age of nineteen. They said I should always be in control of where I was going and who I was going with. If I had my own car I would be in control of who I kept company with.

Mommy and Daddy said: remember this,
Sin will take you to places where you don't want to go.
It makes you do things you don't want to do.
And it keeps you longer than you want to stay.

I John 4:4,
You, dear children, are from God and have overcome them, because the one who is in you is greater than the one who is in the world. They are from the world and therefore speak from the viewpoint of the world, and the world listens to them. We are from God and whoever knows God listens to us. But, whoever is not from God does not listen to us. This is how we recognize the Spirit of Truth from the Spirit of falsehood.

Most of these reality shows are not giving our young people the right message about life.

They are glorifying sin and condoning sinful behavior.

But if a person does not know God's Word he cannot live by God's Word and makes up his own righteousness.

CHAPTER 26

GOD SAYS: AVOID TOO MUCH FOOD AND WINE

Proverbs 23:20,

Do not join those who drink too much wine or gorge themselves on meat, for drunkards and gluttons become poor, and drowsiness clothes them in rags.
Who has bloodshot eyes? Those who linger over wine when it sparkles in a cup and goes down smoothly, in the end it bites like a snake and poisons like a viper.

Proverbs 23:33,
Your eyes will see strange sights and your mind imagine confusing things. You will be like one sleeping on the high seas.

Proverbs 23:35,
They hit me, you will say, but I'm not hurt!
They beat me, but I don't feel it. When will I wake up, so I can find another drink?

Avoid Adultery:
God says, talk to your children about adultery and gangs:

Proverbs 5:1,
My son, pay attention to my wisdom, listen well to my words of insight, that you may maintain discretion.

Proverbs 5:3,
For the lips of an adulteress woman drip honey, and her speech is smoother than oil.

Proverbs 7:14,

The old man saw the young man going to the prostitutes" house when she said, "I have fellowship offerings at home. I have covered my bed with colored linens from Egypt. I have perfumed my bed. Come, let's drink deep of love till morning."

Proverbs 7:21,

With persuasive words she led him astray.

Proverbs 7:31,

All at once he followed her like an ox going to the slaughter, little knowing it will cost him his life.

Proverbs 7:26,

Many are the victims she has brought down.

Jeremiah 3:6,

You have the brazen look of a prostitute: yet you refuse to blush with shame.

God says: Avoid gangs

Proverbs 1:10,

My son, if sinners entice you, do not give in to them.

If they say, come along with us: Let's lie in wait for someone's blood, let's waylay some harmless soul: let's swallow them alive, like the grave.

10:13,

We will get all sorts of valuable things and fill our houses with plunder:
Throw in your lot with us, and we will share a common purse.

10:15,

My son, do not go along with them, do not set foot on their paths; for their feet rush into sin, and they are swift to shed blood.

These men lie in wait for their own blood; they way lay only themselves; such is the end of all who go after ill-gotten gain. It takes away the lives of those who get it.

CHAPTER 27

BE SOMEBODY IN CHRIST

Rev. M.M. Peace was my pastor at Monumental Baptist Church of Philadelphia for the first 50 years of my life. When I graduated from high school in 1959, he preached a sermon to all of the high school graduates. Many were leaving to go off to college.

He said to the parents "Stop telling your children to go to college to be somebody. That's not the purpose of college. In college you will learn a trade or skill that you can build a career on."

"But if you weren't somebody when you went into college, you won't be somebody when you come out of college."

Parents it is your job to build their character and integrity before they ever leave home, and that mainly depends on the way they have seen you walk in front of them.

Children may not always do what you tell them to do, but they will do what they see you do.

"Intelligence and character is the goal of education."

—Martin Luther King

Remember,
We have two natures: a carnal nature and a divine nature, the one we feed is the one that grows. Yes, there is a heaven and a hell. Each of us should decide now where we want to spend eternity. But, as for me and my house, we will serve the Lord.

CHAPTER 28

OUR FOREPARENTS: OUR FOREFRUNNERS

It was the spirit and faith of our fore parents that kept them going, despite the odds. They educated themselves when it was against the law to learn to read.

They hid in the woods, each other's houses and in the basement of churches to teach and educate each other. They would build their churches by asking each one to bring a brick. Some of those churches are still standing today.

Our forefathers established over one hundred colleges more than one hundred and twenty years ago that are still in existence today.

Men like Dr. Benjamin Mays who grew up on a farm plowing mules, attending a one-room schoolhouse became President of Morehouse College for more than forty years. Dr. Mays and the presidents of all of the other black colleges educated our people. They led them to believe that there is nothing that they cannot do.

Most black people seventy years old or older graduated from black colleges. Many of our lawyers, doctors, engineers, scientist and ministers came through black colleges and made contributions to society that changed the world, like Dr. Martin Luther King. It was our black lawyers from black colleges that enforced our civil rights laws.

Many of our inventors never went to college. We are an intelligent people and our circumstances have not been able to keep us back. Like my Daddy always said, "Mr. Got to have will make you think that there is nothing that you cannot do," it creates an environment of ingenuity. We as parents have to help our children connect the dots between the spirit of our forefathers and the challenges that they face today.

Not only is it still relevant it is also encouraging.

CHAPTER 29

CHURCH

My church Monumental Baptist Church is 190 years old. It was started in the home of Rev. George Black, with six people. I was told that it served as the Underground Railroad during slavery. I am proud to be a member. This is also where I learned black history and developed pride in myself as a black woman.

What a legacy of faith to pass down from one generation to another. My grandmother Mary Drummond, my aunt Sula Askew and her husband Henry Askew joined my church around 1930.

My parents joined the church in 1935. My brother was born in 1937 and I was born in 1941. My father would be 119 years old if he was living now and my mother would be 109. So, there have now been six generations that have attended my church including my two great-granddaughters. Members of my church now in their 80's and 90's who were friends with my parents and they remember when my parents joined Monumental Baptist Church. I was 27 years old when my father died, and I only knew him as Daddy. But there are men in my church today who can tell me my father's views on the Black man's state in America and his thoughts on politics, religion, social justice and family. My father-mentored men like Deacon Albert Avant and Rev. Junius Ploughman.

I do remember my dad counseling other young men when they were thinking about leaving their wife and children. My father would say, "It's cheaper to keep her and I'm not only talking about money."

Psalms 1:1, "Do Not Sit In The Counsel Of The Ungodly."

Deacons Of The Church:

Daddy was a deacon and a counselor in our church. The elders of the church felt that it was their responsibility to counsel and hold young men accountable for their families as the head of the household. My father was not perfect. He made some mistakes in his youth. He had a secret that he took to his grave. We just found out that we had an older brother 18 years ago. He found us and we became the best of friends.

But daddy grew and matured and saw the errors of his ways. He acknowledged his wrong by living right and giving young people good Christian advice. He let my brother know that he was going to be the one accountable for his family's welfare regardless to what was going on in his marriage. He said, "You're the adult. Why should your children pay the price? If you can't take it then how can they take it?" Daddy did not want forms of dysfunction to be passed from one generation to another. As parents grow and understand the dysfunction in their families they need to say, "Well, it stops right here. I am not going to let this problem or philosophy be passed onto another generation because it is not healthy."

My brother left his wife and two children one time. He was on his way to get an apartment. My father said, "No, you are not, you cannot afford two places and you will pay the bills at home and take care of your children." My brother started to tell him their problems. My dad said, "I tried to tell you that before you got married at nineteen." You said, "Oh, it doesn't always have to be like that." "Now you have to stay until the youngest child is eighteen years old." Dad told him, "Get out of my car. Go in your house and don't come back out. Make it easy on yourself by trying harder to get along. It will be sad if you stay miserable for the next thirteen years." My brother, Milton and his beautiful wife Barbara have now been married 57 years.

Deaconess of the church:

My mother was a deaconess in the church and she sat on the mother's board. They felt that it was their responsibility to counsel the young women in the church and hold them accountable for their behavior. My mother has girlfriends in our church today that she used to mentor. These women started mentoring me after my mother died when I was fifty years old. I have never outgrown the need for the advice of an elder, they have still been down a road that I have to tread. They are in their 90's, I'm in my seventies and I have to step high to walk in their footprints.

My Heroes:

Mrs. Bertha McMurray who still works as a companion for shut-ins, Irene Morgan, and Martha Johnson. They are such fashion plates that the church members still look to see what they are wearing, because they look so sharp. They still have beautiful homes, they travel, and they carry themselves with dignity and pride.

I have family and friends who have lost children, but they never lost their walk with God: Virginia Kenner, Maloy Scott, Clara Taylor, Katie Billups, Bernandette Staley, Dearia Williamson, Barbara Morris. Nellie Smith, Sula Stone, Swanee Waters and Marion Greaves. They are my heroes because I have watched their walk with God and I know they are watching my walk with God. This is what keeps members of the village accountable to each other.

Children need real live heroes in their lives.

John 16: 22 says:

"Now is your time of grief, but I will see you again and you will rejoice and no one will take away your joy.

Wind beneath my wings:

My sisters in Christ are the wind beneath my wings. Some have been lifetime friends. We share the same faith and belief system regarding family and community.

There are some families that I know whose life testimony has strengthened my faith. Beatrice Dent, Trudy Mitchell, Pat George, Ann Cothran, Peggy Garvin, Dearia Williamson, Marie Weston, Pearl Smith, Elaine Brooks, Rebecca Taylor, Bertha Scott, Lea Rhone, Sandra Williams, Anita Shaw, and Deidra King.

I know that their prayers were holding me when my mother was sick and I couldn't pray. Their prayers were holding me for the six weeks when I was sick, but had not been diagnosed yet and through my most recent surgeries.

CHAPTER 30

VISIONARIES

I heard my parents tell stories about men and women who did not have children, but would pay the college tuition for other young people to go to college. I know for a fact that Mrs. Marie F. Bowes who was a schoolteacher and superintendent of our Sunday School sent three young ladies from our church to college and it could have been more in her family or community in the 1950's.

In the seventies, my church started a college scholarship fund for the children. It is still in operation. Many of the children are now adults and grandparents themselves.

Our church is in the so-called "ghetto," but we still have values and standards for our children. We gave our children faith and hope. We taught them that they were an asset to themselves, their families, and their community.

They have become doctors, airline pilots, corporate CEO's, equal employment specialist, mechanical, structural, and chemical engineers, movie producers, real estate tycoons, politicians, nurses, teachers, professors, school counselors, photographers, social workers, psychologist, radiation technicians, medical directors, ministers, musicians, graphic artists, audio technicians, and most recently a hospital medical director for the department of physical therapy.

Now some of them are leaders in our church and in the churches where they have relocated and some have sent money back to continue supporting the scholarship fund.

Our young leaders today are teaching our children audio technology, how to develop web sites and to create videos of their programs and how to advertise their programs on radio. They are learning all aspects of church leadership through their own children's church, with a real emphasis on public speaking. They have planted a garden and they are learning how to eat and live healthy.

Everything you need to survive is in the village. Single parents, yes you can raise responsible children in a village. Example: There was one family of children in our church, the Hardy's, that participated in everything in the church, their school, and their community. They lived in the projects and I don't know if their mother ever had a car. Their mother worked night shifts and weekends, so I never got to know her, but I knew who she was and what she stood for by the character of her children. Their mother had faith, values, and standards for her children. They understood why she worked so hard for them. The last thing they wanted to do was hurt or disappoint their mother.

The two young women became successful businesswomen and their brother is a commercial airline pilot.

CHAPTER 31

MARRIAGE: GOD'S FAMILY PLAN

God has a family plan. Circumstances in life, sometimes beyond our control, keep us from staying on course. But we are to never stop struggling toward or aiming for his plan. His plan is what is true, what is noble, what is right. The family should love each other as Jesus loves the church. The husband should be the role model of love and forgiveness.

Husband:

Believes God's word and know that God listens to his heart. He knows that God will protect, provide, forgive and guide him and his house to joy, peace, happiness and success as long as he is obedient to God's word.

Wife:

Respects her husband because she knows that God is going to hold the man accountable for his family's welfare. She knows that her husband listens to her heart. Therefore, he is going to be a role model of love for his children and protect, forgive, and provide her every need to guide her to joy, peace, happiness and success in whatever she wants to do or be, just as God is helping him.

Children:

Respect and obey their parents because they know that their parents are listening to their hearts. They know they are going to love, provide, forgive and guide them to peace, happiness, joy and a successful life.

Exodus 20:6 says,

"God will show mercy unto thousands that love and keep his commandments."

I learned the principles above at Christian Stronghold Baptist Church's Biblical Counseling course in 1990.

My pastor, Rev. Dr. Wendell Mapson Jr. from Monumental Baptist Church of Phila. Says

"God is our heavenly father, but he knows that every child needs an earthly father who is Godly, and will be obedient to him by trusting him. That's why God chose Joseph to be the father of Jesus. Matthew 1–2.

There are couples that live by God's family plan.

Couple #1: Working Together, being of one mind and one spirit.

I know of one couple that lives according to God's plan. They were married five years when they had their first child. The wife decided to take a new job when her baby was 4 months old. After 6 months of probation, she was offered a great promotion. However, they said to her, "We have a position that would be great for you, but it requires traveling, and we know that you have a little baby."

Mother states that, "The baby has a Daddy who knows how to take care of her. He knows that when he feeds himself the baby is hungry too. When he bathes himself the baby also needs a bath. I know that I can take the job because they will be just fine." She started traveling one week out of every month, covering five states in five days.

He continued working and taking the baby to a babysitter. After six years, another baby came along and they continued their routine. He says, "The key is organization and keeping a routine." When she would return on Friday, the house was clean and the children kept up with all of their activities.

A typical Saturday looked like this when the baby was young. He would get up and put three meats in the oven, three starches, and three vegetables. He would put clothes in the washer and dryer, and clean the house. His wife and oldest daughter would go shopping for the food and clothes they needed for the house. Mom and daughter would also go to the hairdresser. By 4 o'clock, the family was free for family time on Saturday nights and all day Sunday, and everything was ready for the following workweek.

His wife says, "It is because of his support that she has been able to move up the corporate ladder."

He said, "he got it from his momma, who was single."

Couple #2—Be evenly yoked

I had a neighbor who had five children in a one-bedroom apartment. The mother stayed home and the father worked two jobs. The children say their mother was very strict about their academic education. Their father was very strict about their spiritual education. He always told them to, "seek ye first the kingdom of God and His righteousness and all other things will be added unto you." Matthew 6:33.

He eventually moved them to a beautiful house and had two more children. I only kept up with the first four children.

#1) The oldest son is a Professor of Theology.

#2) The second son made a career in the army and he is now retired.

#3) The oldest daughter cleaned offices at night when she was in high school. She went to college and majored in environmental engineering and business administration. She now owns a company that cleans ships all over the world.

#4) The second daughter owns a company that sells black art to museums and art galleries around the world.

The mother and father are now world travelers trying to keep up with their children.

Proverbs 23:18,
    "There is surely a future for you and your hope will not be cut off."

So, don't lose hope when times are hard, you have to hold on to your faith and believe that you will rise up out of your present situation.

CHAPTER 32

AMAZING MEN

There are some amazing men in my village. I am in awe at the strength and courage that they have. The following are just a few good men who lead, provide, protect, and stepped up to the plate when their family was in crisis. They are living life according to God's family plan.

#1) Khalin:

This is my cousin Pat's only child. Pat moved from Philadelphia to Houston, Texas. Two years ago, she was on a plane flying from Houston to Philadelphia to visit her family here. She was having trouble with her knee and she put a knee brace on. The knee brace restricted the blood flow and caused a blood clot to form in her knee. When she got to Philly and took it off the blood clot moved to her lungs and she had a massive heart attack.

The doctor's told us she was brain dead and she was just a vegetable and we should take her off life support. Her son Khalin could not get her insurance to fly her home on a medical airline. Plus, no hospital there wanted to accept a patient that was already brain dead. Her son who is a very quiet, reserved person and would never ask anyone for anything went to everyone he knew and raised the money needed to fly her home. I sat with her and talked to her everyday while her son flew back and forth trying to get her home. Six weeks later, I said, "Hello Pat" and she said, "Hello." A few minutes later, her son called and said that the airline was willing to fly her home and he found a hospital there to accept her. I put her on the phone and she said "Hello" to her son.

After he got her home, she would show a little progress and her doctors and the rehab hospital would always say, "That's as far as she can go." He got his brothers from his fraternity to go with him to take up all the carpet in her house and lay down new hardwood floors to accommodate her hospital bed on wheels and her wheelchair. They also built a handicap ramp up to the house.

She stayed in a nursing home for thirty days and he moved her back to her own house. He moved in with her, continued to work every day, brought in all the services she needed as she progressed along. He also worked and held onto his wife, children and responsibilities at home.

She is now living alone. I went to visit her March 10th, 2014. She cooked and served me all of my meals and we just hung out doing the girlie things we used to do in the good old days.

When I arrived in Houston, Texas the taxi cab driver asked if I was visiting. I told him, "I am coming to see my cousin after two years." I told him her story. The cab fare was thirty dollars. He would not let me pay him. He said, "God told him to deliver me to my cousin." He said, "All I want to see is her to open the door and wave at me. He was standing in the middle of the street waving at her when she opened the door. She waved back and came down on the porch to hug me. He got in his cab and drove away. I guess this was a testimony that he needed to hear.

#2) Cousin Paul and Allen:

Paul was his parents, Jerry and Willie's only child. His mother's two sisters Massey and Remel who did not have children were like a mother to him also. Paul had a best friend name, Allen. His house was directly behind Paul's. He was also an only child. So, they became best friends. Everything Paul's family planned for him they included Allen. And Allen's family was the same way with Paul. Allen was considered Massey and Remel's adopted nephew.

Paul became a Catholic Priest in Atlantic City, New Jersey. Allen married Gladys and they have two children. When Paul's Aunt Remel took sick and became bound to a wheel chair, Allen took over. He found and coordinated all of the services Remel needed to remain in her house for seven years.

Gladys would cook her meals and he took them to Remel every day. He also worked and took care of his wife, children, his mother, and his home, neglecting no one in the process.

Shortly after, Remel died. Paul's mother Jerry took sick. Paul took her to live with him in Atlantic City. He had great responsibility as a priest, but she was not neglected in any way. He brought all of the services she needed into the home and he supervised her care.

Paul's mother lived with him for five years. When he brought his Aunt Massey to Atlantic City for his mother's funeral, he realized that she could no longer live alone. He kept his Aunt for five years also.

#3) Mr. Jones:

Mr. Jones lived in my village. He had six children and a wife who was sick. He had five boys and one girl, and my son would visit them sometimes on the weekends. All of them were mentors to my son. Mr. Jones worked two full-time jobs to provide for his family. Mrs. Jones would often take charge of discipline when her husband was not at home.

When he arrived home they would talk about the issues and decide whether a joint meeting time was required. They were dedicated to ensuring that their children were respectful and had a love for God.

Mr. and Mrs. Jones five children became ministers. I couldn't attend Mrs. Jones funeral, however, I went to Mr. Jones funeral. I saw four sons, one daughter, and some grandsons walking behind their father's coffin in their ministerial robes while the other grandsons perched their grandfather's coffin on their shoulders and carried him out. This was such an awesome sight, I could only cry and sing, hallelujah!

#4) Terrance

I had a friend named Lillian. She had one son Terrance. She lived in Philadelphia. Her son lived in Florida. She had a stroke that left her speechless and paralyzed. Terrance moved her to Florida with him. He searched and found the best nursing home he could find to meet her needs. He then moved to an apartment across the street from the nursing home. He had to continue working and he knew that she could not get the care and therapy she needed if she lived with him.

But every evening when he got off from work and she had her dinner, he would bring her to sit on the balcony with him in his apartment until bedtime.

He found a church that was on the first floor with no steps. He would dress her up in pretty dresses and hats, and take her to church every Sunday. He would park her wheelchair and carry her in his arms to her seat. Meanwhile, he was still a devoted single father and grandfather. His mother-in-law was such a great support to him when his children were young that when she got sick he took care of her too. She did get well, however, and returned to her own home.

Terrance, unfortunately, got cancer and died recently. I only hope that he got the care that he gave everyone else. I talked to him one time in Florida. He sounded very positive at the time, but he did lose his battle.

#5) Ronald

I had a friend named Carol; her husband's name is Ronald. Carol became bed-ridden with multiple sclerosis and remained paralyzed for 35 years. She could not move anything on her body, but her eyes and her tongue. Mentally, she remained conscious and aware of everything going on around her and in the world. I enjoyed visiting with her because we could discuss current events and talk about the good old days.

Her husband Ronald refused to put her in a nursing home. He gave her the best of care. Her hair was always done and she was always dressed very nicely. She was a school administrator for the board of education before she got sick. Ronald enjoyed inviting her old co-workers and sorority sisters in to visit with her. They raised their two sons to be successful professionals. One of the main reasons he kept her home, he wanted her to be involved in guiding them and showing them her love and support. Carol died about three years ago. Ronald still lives in their large house, basking in the success of his grandchildren. Ronald knows that if he had done things differently the family would not be bonded the way they are today.

#6) John

I take my hat off to my cousin Barbara's husband, John. She has been seriously ill with multiple sclerosis for many years. The love and devotion that he shows and gives relentlessly is mind blowing, while raising a wonderful son and beautiful daughter, who are college graduates.

There are men in our village who know and live by God's family plan. They have great challenges in their lives, but they are never thrown off track as far as their love and responsibilities to their families are concerned. Television should portray the strong men in our communities and the intact families they are nurturing.

CHAPTER 33

WELFARE, SCHOOL AND WORK

Welfare:

I started college when I was thirty-seven years old. I finished a four-year curriculum in three years. I owned a duplex apartment house. I lived on the first floor. I did not need cash assistance from welfare because I had rent from the apartment. However, I was eligible for food stamps and a medical card. I was so grateful for the help that I wrote a letter to the department of public welfare thanking them for helping me. I told them my plan to graduate in three years and the date that I would stop needing their help. God was with me. I found a job as a medical social worker the same month I graduated from Antioch University. I wrote a letter and told them to discontinue my benefits on the exact day that I had predicted I would get off welfare. I thanked them because their assistance enabled me to go to school.

Phenomenal Women:

I learned as much from other students as I learned from my books, in undergraduate and graduate school. When I was in undergraduate school I was going to school full-time, working part-time and doing my internship. I would run home and feed my children, pick up my mother to babysit and go to school at night. One night, I told a lady sitting next to me name Harriet that I was so tired, I didn't know how much longer I could continue at this pace.

#1) Harriet

She told me that she worked full-time and went to school part-time. She had eleven children, a sick husband, and a sick daughter at home. I never complained to her again, but I paid close attention to her strength and tenacity.

#2) Ruth

I worked with a woman named Ruth. She was a receptionist on my job. She had twelve children. When I met her, ten had completed college. Two were doctors at Children's Hospital. She had two children at home. When the twelfth child started Temple University she went to college with her and they graduated together.

She said, her first husband had died and left her with seven children and her second husband died and left her with five more children. They never had more than three bedrooms and five beds. They all wore cardboard in their shoes at times. Even though they were poor, Jesus Christ, education, and music was her first priorities in their lives.

#3) Frances

When I went to graduate school I became a lifetime friend with Frances. She had ten children and her two youngest children were in undergraduate school.

#4) A Lecturer

I went to a lecture and the speaker had eleven children. She had just received her Doctor's degree and she was a professor of linguistics.

CHAPTER 34

A BROKEN MARRIAGE
DOES NOT NECESSARILY MEAN
BROKEN CHILDREN

My son:

My son has been married twenty-five years to a wonderful God-fearing wife, Antoinette. They have two daughters; Ebony, 21 and Destiny, 14 years old. He is now pastor of a church and his main passion is counseling single mothers with sons. However, he and his wife counsel individuals and families together to give a male and female Christian perspective and as a measure of safety.

Damon wouldn't read to two people in Sunday School when he was 15 years old. His teacher didn't think he could read. He said he couldn't read in front of people.

When he preached his trial sermon, he preached to 2,000 people for 1 solid hour without notes. They had to peel me off my seat.

When he was installed as Pastor of his new church, he invited his father. His father sat in the back of the church. I invited him to sit up front with me. Damon said it made him proud to introduce his mother and father together to the congregation. When the service was over we had to peel him off his seat. He was in awe. There were over 500 people in the congregation, twenty-five ministers laid hands on him in prayer and there were over 100 voices in the choir from churches all over Texas. My ex-husband became a Muslim after we divorced. But he was truly impressed with the outpouring of love shown to his son.

He was proud of the house my son built with a bedroom and bathroom for me.

My son's theme for life is:
    "I've been saved to serve others."

My son's sermon for Mother's Day was: "You Got It From Your Momma."

2 Timothy 1:3,
This was Paul's letter to Timothy telling him that he gets his faith from his mother Eunice and his Grandmother Lois." He compared Timothy with himself and said he got his faith from his mother Mary and his grandmothers, Lenora and Dorothy.

My daughter:
My daughter Kenya has always been a strong black woman. She has had many setbacks and disappointments as a single mother of two daughters, Kendra 27 and Kyra 18 years old. But Kenya finished college; she has the job and the house of her dreams.

Every time she got laid off a good job, it was mainly due to government subcontracting. She would get up and come back more determined to reach whatever goal she was aiming for at the time she got knocked down.

My daughter is a minister in her church and she has a special ministry for single mothers and parents who have lost their children.

The main theme in her life is:
"Don't die in the winter, hold on until your change comes."

Proverbs 24:16,
"For though the righteous fall seven times, they rise again, but the wicked stumble when calamity strikes."

I learned from watching my daughter that what Paul says is true, "It is when she is at her weakest point that she is her strongest." 2 Corinthians 12:10

My granddaughter's and great-granddaughter's:
I have four granddaughters and they are all youth leaders in their churches.

I have two great-granddaughters Kayliana is 7 years old and Kapri is 5 years old. They are also grounded in the Word. If they know someone in the room is sick they will lay hands on them and pray for them with just a moment's notice.

Exodus 20:6,
"But showing love to a thousand generations of those who love me and keep my commandments."

CHAPTER 35

JOIN A COALITION: DON'T ISOLATE YOURSELF

When you are struggling with a serious situation even a life-changing situation join a coalition. Do not isolate yourself. Whatever it is, you are not going through it alone. There's someone out there who knows and understands how you feel. If it's medical join a group for heart problems, cancer, or whatever. If it's a social problem, find a group who has the same concerns and form a coalition. Be active on your block, a parent-teacher association, or with your union on your job. There are committees forming now to fight for raising the minimum wage. If this is a serious issue for you, join the fight.

Encourage your children to be active in city, state, and federal organizations that could address their concerns. City and statewide sports competitions, science, health fairs, and career symposiums. Churches of various denominations have conferences for children that address their interests, problems and concerns. We cannot allow our children to focus on what they do not have. When they are outgoing and active they can see that whatever their problems are at this time will one day be over. (And this too shall pass.)

Strongholds in the Village:

There is a myth that black people do not stick together like other races.

There are organizations that have been the strongholds in our village. They have brought us together cohesively and helped us to keep our history, values, customs and traditions intact, developing dignity and pride in ourselves as a people.

Churches, NAACP, Urban League, Masons, Eastern Stars, Fraternities, Sororities, The Links and Jack and Jill Clubs, Boys and Girls Clubs of America, Police Athletic Leagues, Community Recreation Centers, and the YWCA and YMCA, The Philadelphia Academy of Cadets, (a military drill team) The Moles,

Black Theatres and Dance Companies and National Associations. The Philadelphia Tribune, Ebony, Jet, and Essence Magazines and Black Radio Stations have kept us abreast with life in our village.

I salute black foster and adoption agencies that supported our children and families, and held them together through difficult times. Such as the Women's Christian Alliance who held on for more than a hundred years, and Southern Baptist Homes. Sister Falaka Fattah is over 80 years old and was in the mission field keeping the House of Umoja open for boys who were homeless.

I belong to the local and National Association of Black Social Workers. My brother, Ben, belonged to the National Association of Black Pharmacists. My sister-in-law Jackie belongs to the National Association of Black Nurses. National Conferences give you a chance to meet other professionals from around the country and the world to discuss legislation and policies that affect the livelihood of all people across the diaspora. It also gives a voice and access to your political representative's in city, state, and federal government.

It is because of these bonds that we have been able to stay together and stand up against Jim Crow, separatism, segregation, racism, prejudice, discrimination and injustice.

CHAPTER 36

LOWS AND HIGHS OF RETIREMENT

Lowest Points:

The lowest point of retirement is watching friends your age lose their health and pass away. I've lost six friends in the last 2 years. I've sat with them and held some of them until they took their last breathe. I bought the clothes for two of them for their funerals. It was hard because I can remember buying formal wear and us shopping together for banquets, weddings and cruises.

I had a friend Evelyn who died in August of 2013; we sat together in church for over 30 years. A month later, I was sitting in my seat crying because I missed her so much. My friend Becky tapped me on my shoulder and she said, "Don't grieve too long because you are going to get your turn too, just enjoy today."

I had to laugh and I told her she was crazy. But it's true, as hard and as painful as it is, we have to allow ourselves to get caught up in the pleasantries of each day.

High points of retirement:

I have two friends who have relocated since retirement. My friend Marcella has built a new home in Florida. She invited me to go with her to pick the lot and design her house. We are enjoying it immensely in Florida. Cheryl is still in the process of building her house and it is so much fun helping her design her house from the pavement to the back yard and plan a whole new life for herself.

Free to travel:

My friend Swanee called me one day and said "A cruise ship is leaving NY on September 8th, let's be on it." I said "Okay." I had to call her back to ask her where we were going and how much it cost.

Traveling gives you a whole new perspective on life. You can see a difference in lifestyles, customs, and culture traveling just in the United States, but especially abroad. You also find out how much you have in common with other people in other cultures.

CHAPTER 37

TRAVEL BROADENS YOUR PERSPECTIVE: UNDERSTANDING THE HUMAN SPIRIT

Four of my most memorable trips were to Egypt, Ghana, South Africa, and Trinidad.

Egypt:

Dr. La Francis Rose, a professor of Black History at Rutgers University in New Brunswick, New Jersey took a group of Black Women and one man on a 27-day tour of Egypt and Ghana.

I visited the Pyramids in Egypt. Sometimes, we would walk twenty stories down into the pyramids. The Egyptians have their whole life story carved into stone. The colors are as bright as if they were painted yesterday. Anthropologist are still trying to figure out how they built the pyramids which are large block stones, one sitting on top of the other, and this was all done before the birth of Christ (B.C.). In the countryside people are still riding camels, herding sheep, and living in one-room huts with their animals. We rode camels and cruised the Nile River at night.

Coptic Christians Persecuted:

I visited the Coptic Church in Egypt. The tour guide said, "That Coptic Church was built on the site where Mary and Joseph hid the baby Jesus in Egypt."

He said, "There is a large congregation of Coptic Christians throughout the Arab Republic of Egypt in the Middle East, Asia and North Africa."

In the month of March 2015, 29 Coptic Christians were beheaded and ISIS abducted 250 for their Christian beliefs.

Ghana:

I visited the Amina slave castles in the Cape Coast of Ghana. It is hard to believe the philosophies and strategies that are used when one nation wants to enslave and colonize another country, to steal their diamonds and mineral resources, to name a few.

When I went to the Amina slave castle the tour guide took us through the dungeon where the slaves were kept captive. We ended up at the "The Door of No Return." He said they named it that because when we went down the planks to the slave ship they did not think they would ever see us again. Many of the women were pregnant by their slave masters when they got on the ship.

We held hands, prayed, and cried together. The tour guide said that it is good to know that we know this is our legacy and we care enough to come back to our homeland and learn our heritage.

The National Council For Black Studies Annual Conference was held in Ghana while I was there. The attendees were mostly from Europe, the U.S.A., other African countries and the Caribbean. I got a chance to sit down and have a conversation at lunchtime with Maya Angelou, who lectured at the conference. She lived in Ghana when she was married. She helped Dr. Kwame Nkrumah plan the over throw of Colonial Rule on March 6,1957. She also lectured at the DuBois Center in Accra Ghana. She stated that Dr. Nkrumah attended Lincoln University, where many Africa leaders attended college in the United States.

She was in Ghana to register her grandson in the University of Ghana.

There were black educators from all over the world studying and emphasizing the importance of having black history, (Pan African Studies) included in educational curriculums around the world.

I also ate lunch and talked with the following historians from the United States.
Dr. John Henrik Clarke, historian and scholar of Pan-American Studies

Dr. Leonard Jefferies, a professor at a N.Y. College,

Stokely Carmichael, a member of SNCC (Student Nonviolent Coordinating Committee) and a member of the Black Panther Party, he also started the black power movement in the United States in the 1960s. We talked about his life in Ghana.

Bob Law, N.Y. radio talk show host and Dr. Kwanza Kunjufu, author of the book "The conspiracy to destroy black boys." They both presented workshops on the importance of Black Talk radio stations. I followed their tour of Ghana when they lectured at night.

We had a five-hour layover in Egypt when we flew from Ghana to Egypt and waited for our next flight to the United States together. So, I had the undivided attention of Dr. Kunjufu and Bob Law for lunch and dinner.

South Africa:

I went to South Africa with Dr. Ian Jacobs, an administrator and professor at Rutgers University of Camden after Mandela became president, two years after apartheid ended.

We went to see the prison where Mandela was imprisoned for many years on Robbens Island. It was not open as a museum at that time.

Rutgers University sent Dr. Ian Jacobs there to discuss strategies for dismantling apartheid policies in three of their universities.

We went to Namibia, South Africa first, to visit the University of Namibia. There was an all black college just two years old in Winhoek, Namibia.

Rutgers University established an exchange program for their staff and students between Rutgers University and Namibia University. They also discussed some of the legislation and apartheid policies that were still in place in South Africa limiting their growth.

We also went on safaris in Etosha National Park Reserve and we climbed sand dunes at the Cape Point and the Cape of Good Hope. It was the most exhilarating experience in my life.

Then we flew to Cape Town, South Africa. We went to the University of The Western Cape and saw their first integrated parade.

One of the main purposes of the trip: visit the University of Stellenbosch which is equal to Harvard, to discuss strategies for dismantling apartheid policies that were still keeping blacks from attending. Example: Their undergraduate studies were written in Afrikan, a language they designed for white Germans only. So, black children could not attend. Their graduate programs were in English. They brought in their one and only black student to meet us and to let us know they were interested in integration. He went to undergraduate school in London and then came back to Cape Town for graduate school.

We stayed in the best hotels and ate in the finest restaurants and we astonished the guest because we were the first blacks to patronize their venues. Only black tourists could afford to stay in these places.

I'm not black:

When my friend Veronica and I were flying from Namibia to Cape Town, South Africa, we met a young man, named Kevin Poggenpoel on the plane. Kevin was light-skinned and he said that, "I'm not black." "The light-skinned people in South Africa were never under apartheid. They were the workforces. They were allowed to work, go to school, and buy property, but there was a glass ceiling that determined how far they could go up the ladder of success, until apartheid ended."

Kevin invited Veronica and I to his house for dinner. He invited his mother and father to give us their history in South Africa. He said that, "It was the black people who were banished to the bush not the colored people." However, this was the first time their family had ever entertained black people in their home. His parents said they were glad to live long enough to see integrated schools and hopefully integrated communities one day.

A person's color was their badge under apartheid in South Africa as it was for all black people of color during slavery and Jim Crow in the United States.

Father to son: angry with God

Kevin's father said that he and his brothers were all fisherman. They made plenty of money. It was their dream to send their sons to college and open a chain of seafood restaurants; they had the money for both.

Kevin majored in Business and some studied to be culinary chefs. But they could not get the licensing they needed to open a business. They didn't even need loans from the bank, but they hit that glass ceiling for colored people.

Kevin could not find a job with his business degree. He had to accept a job as a welder working in the bottom of ships. His father said that, "It hurt him to see his son working those dirty jobs in the bottom of a ship with a college degree." Kevin had to learn all of the trades to keep a job. His cousins did not do well in the job market either. Daddy said he was disappointed.

Angry with God:

His father said that, "he was angry with God because he felt that the White man came to South Africa with the Bible when they had the land. Now, they have the Bible and the White man has the land."

But God let him live to see where their "Setback was their Set-up for their Comeback."

After apartheid ended, Kevin was appointed the President of the first trade school open to Blacks in Cape town, South Africa, because of his business degree and his experience in building trades. That's why he was in Namibia when we met him. He was recruiting students to attend the first trade school for blacks in Cape Town, South Africa.

Kevin was also studying to be a minister in the Anglo-Saxon Church under Archbishop Desmond TuTu.

Kevin's father says, "He is no longer angry with God because he can see the path God has laid out for him and his family."

The father said that, "He can also see what he was teaching his children when they were young when he was emphasizing the importance of their education." He would tell them, "When equality and emancipation comes and the playing field is leveled, I want you to be ready to play."

After Mandela became President of South Africa, the black people started moving into towns to look for work. They lived in tin shacks and their living conditions were deplorable. The government built cement huts for some of the people migrating from the bush. They said that, "It was all they needed because that's what they were accustomed to."

Coming to America:

Kevin brought his family to Philadelphia to visit Veronica Rucker and I two years later. We exchanged stories on the struggle out of slavery and through the era of emancipation.

The New Apartheid:

Kevin and I talked about the "new apartheid" that will emerge after this period of reconstruction in South Africa, like Jim Crow, segregation and minimum wage has done in America.

It will occur in a different form in South Africa, but most societies want the majority of the working class to earn less than a living wage, and they will design a system, disguised under another name and formed to keep the lower class in their place.

Middle class looks the same around the world:

His twelve-year-old daughter, Kim looked just like my twelve-year-old grand-daughter Kendra. They liked the same style clothes, music, movies, and dances. We were surprised that they had so much in common. We learned that middle class values and lifestyle are almost the same everywhere.

South Africa did not have museums for the plight and legacy of Blacks at that time. Kevin took his family to the Black history museum in Philadelphia, Washington, D.C. and the Black Wax Museum in Baltimore, MD.

It was in America that Kevin and his family learned the history of Africans in Africa and America, and how we were scattered throughout the world.

He collected many books and artifacts to take back to his father and mother, and his community.

Kevin also enjoyed my experiences in Egypt, Ghana, South Africa, and Trinidad. I gave him books and artifacts from all of my trips.

He was really impressed with his visit to the Franklin institute of Science.

Trinidad:

The National Alliance of Black Social Workers held their international conference in Trinidad in 1994. We would convene in various countries to look at the social systems impacting the welfare of families.

Our main concern for that conference was the high rate of teenage suicide. Their school system at that time only provided a free education until the eighth grade. The children would then take a test that would determine if they could go further in school.

If they did not pass the test and their parents could not afford to pay for high school, then they could not go. This put a lot of pressure on children up until the eighth grade. If they did not pass the test the parents would be very disappointed in their children and would often give up on them. The children would be ashamed and depressed. Their feelings of hopelessness led to a high rate in crime and suicide for teenagers.

So, we looked at strategies of establishing a broader curriculum of Social Work in their undergraduate and graduate programs at the University of Trinidad. To expand their education on early childhood and adolescent development and the impact of these antiquated policies to the detriment of families.

It was another way of creating a poor working class of people for the system. Just like apartheid did in South Africa. Slavery and Jim Crow did in America, and continues to do today with minimum wage. It keeps widening the gap between "The Have and The Have Not's."

We emphasized the necessity of social workers becoming the advocates, lobbyist, politicians and agents for change in Trinidad because we understand the human spirit and the needs of the people.

CHAPTER 38

DON'T TELL YOUR CHILDREN

Kevin surprised me when he said that his children, who were twelve and fifteen years old, did not know the full history of blacks in South Africa because that was not the world that they lived in. It certainly was not taught in school or talked about at home until Mandela's release from prison.

I was angry when he first said it, but then I remembered that my parents and other relatives did not like to talk about their life in the South as sharecroppers, farmers and servants and how they were lynched for minor misdemeanors. My mother's father left to avoid being lynched, but they never heard from him again and so they assumed that he had been caught, but I was grown before they told me their story.

It wasn't until I got older and started reading our history and questioning my parents that I could confirm what I read.

Parenting:

I realize now that most parents from many cultures do shield their children from as much pain and unpleasantness as they can. They don't know that it is important to tell them their history, so that when it comes back in different forms and disguises they will recognize it.

Slavery ended January 1, 1863, but Jim Crow laws and sharecropping were designed to eradicate everything we accomplished through emancipation and the period of reconstruction. The Jim Crow laws prohibited learning because they did not want the sharecropper to count how much they had earned at the end of the year. The landowner would tell them that they were in debt to them if it was a bad year. If it was a good year they would tell them that they broke even because it paid up their back debt.

If they questioned their landowners about their salary, they were hanged.

They never wanted them to have cash available because they would then be able to run away, and so they were still working for free as they did during slavery days. It was against the law to learn how to read because it was another way to keep them from voting or knowing their rights as citizens. If they knew how to read, they would fight for their right to vote.

My parents did not consider this as another form of slavery, but laws were passed so that they could not sell their crops after they purchased their own farms They could only plant the crops that they needed to feed their families. This was another strategy to keep the masses from progressing.

CHAPTER 39

HOLOCAUST SURVIVORS

I recently read an article in the Sunday Inquirer, November 2014

Visiting Yad Vashen, Pop Pop is ready to share.

Author Samantha Farkas got her grandfather, Jakab Farakas, a survivor of Auschwitz-Bukenau, at Yad Vashen, in Jerusalem to return for a visit. They went into the World Center for Holocaust Research and her grandfather looked for himself in pictures and he told her his story as they toured the museum.

Mr. Jakab-Farakas had never told his children his experiences in the holocaust. They knew it was too painful, so they asked her not to bring it up, but he was ready to share it with his second generation.

There is an inscription outside the visitor's center of Yad Voshen, The World Center or Holocaust Research, located in Jerusalem. It reads:

"Has the like of this happened in your days or in the days of your fathers? Tell your children about it, and let your children tell theirs, and their children the next generation."

CHAPTER 40

EXPERIENCING ONE OF THE WONDERS OF THE WORLD

I was flying from Ghana to Egypt on a ten-hour flight. When we were crossing the equator I was sitting in the window seat and the sky was as black as velvet with a full moon seemingly at my fingertips.

I turned to my right to tell the lady sitting next to me to look at the beautiful moon. To my surprise, the sun was shining on my right side and it was daylight.

Midnight on the left side of the plane and daylight on the right side of the plane: It took everything in me to not run up and down the aisle shouting.

I calmed myself down by repeating Psalm 19:1,

"The heavens declare the glory of God, the skies proclaim the work of his hands."

I finished my flight singing to myself, "How Great Thou Art."

CHAPTER 41

RECALIBRATE YOUR LIFE

Paraphrasing:
My pastor Rev. Dr. Wendell J. Mapson, Jr. at Monumental Baptist Church in Philadelphia says, "You have to recalibrate your life."

This is sort of the way our cell phones and GPS towers operate. When you get in your car and turn on your GPS system you do not have to tell them where you are, just say where you want to go and the system will map out your route. If you stay on track with the map you will get to your destination quickly.

But because we are human we get hungry and tired and we want to get off the expressway for some R&R (rest and relaxation). That's the way it is on the expressway of life. Being good, working hard, and staying focused can be exhausting. So, we need to know when to stop, rest, and regroup.

We need to see where we are in route to our destination. How far have we come and how much further do we have to travel to get there? This is good, healthy, and necessary, but your still off track. You have detoured, so get back in your car and turn on the GPS and map out which way you have to go from your present position.

Have you changed your mind?

Have you changed your goals?

Have you decided that it is too far to make it to your previous destination?

No? You're still determined to get there; you have the strength and tenacity to make it. Okay turn to God, I mean turn to your GPS, and your original destination and it will recalibrate the route you need to take to get there from where you are.

Oh! You weren't using God's map. You didn't realize that God has a system in place for you to keep you on track. You have just been traveling an unknown route by yourself, how has it worked for you? The philosophy that you have lived by, is it working? Do you have peace with the journey you have chosen? Do you want to go the rest of the way by yourself?

Remember, you don't know all of the exits on the expressway. If you get off on the wrong exit, you may end up in a dark dangerous place and never find your way back to God's highway.

You're driving the car, but your whole family is in the car with you. Your parents, your wife, and your children, and they have to go wherever you are going.

But it's not too late. If you admit that you are lost, you can always turn to God for directions. He hasn't gone anywhere. He's just waiting for you to ask him for help.

I guess that's what I'm doing by writing this book. I'm looking back through my rearview mirror. I'm asking myself, how I started out, what happened in route to age seventy-four. How many potholes and flat tires have I had along the way? Where do I go from here? Am I tired? Do I just want to coast the rest of the way on a scenic route or do I want to get back on the expressway of life?

I am recalibrating my life, reading my Bible, and depending on the Holy Spirit who dwells within me to guide me onto the next chapter of my life.

This is what we have to do to reclaim our village. Do we like where we are? Do we like what our children are doing? Do we like the methods that we have used and the messages that we are giving our children? If not, we need to stop and recalibrate as a people.

CHAPTER 42

HEALING THE VILLAGE

"Parents train your children in the way they should go and when they are old they will not turn from it," Proverbs 22:6." If they do and they want to come back they will, because they will hear your voice and they will know the way back.

Tell your children how important they are. I think that has been the rock of my foundation. I knew I was loved and that I was important to my family and relatives in my village before I started school.

Teach your children that it is their responsibility to be healthy. It is not only for their well being and the future of their children, but for the prosperity of the village. Remind them that there are young people who look up to them. There are some young persons who think they are important and know it all. It could be a younger brother, sister, cousin or neighbor looking at them. They are role models whether they want to be or not and there's someone out there who cares. So, they should care enough to make a positive influence on those coming behind them.

Let your children know that it is normal and natural to dream, especially, if we are in a bad place at the moment. When we are in a rut, financial or otherwise, dreams keep our hope alive.

Make plans for your life. Set short-term goals and work on them one day at a time. Set long-term goals for yourself and develop a strategy for achieving your goals, but we need at least two more back up plans too. This will cause you to challenge yourself to reach your goals.

Parents we must study and stay ahead of the changing trends. We live in a world system that fluctuates with uncertainty from day to day.

Example:

Because of the impact of technology and social media it is predicted that large shopping malls, casinos, universities, and the post office, to name a few, will be phased out as we know them today. It is scary because we know that those with the least will fall first. It is being predicted the middleclass will eventually disappear and there will only be the rich and the poor.

Man will become so smart that he will self-destruct.

Proverbs 21:13 says,
"If a man shuts his ears to the cry of the poor, he too will cry out and not be answered."

So, where does that leave us?
We need the village more today to survive and be healthy than ever before.

Faith:
We must keep our mind in the game and our hope in Jesus Christ.
We don't know what the future holds, but we do know who holds the future.
A Christian goes from faith to trials to greater faith to greater trials. It is a pilgrimage.

Therefore we all must remember Trinity:
God is the Father: Creator of all things
God is the Son: Who has come to show us the way, the truth, and the light, and no one comes unto the Father except through Jesus Christ.
God the Holy Spirit: Who dwells within us and will comfort us in the time of trouble and will guide us out if only we believe.
As for me, I know that if I had not had tests, I would not have this testimony.

Listen to the voices in your village because minds sharpen minds.

This picture was taken after my ex-husband heard our son preach for the first time. Proverbs 23:13 says "The father of a good man has great joy. May your father and mother be glad, may she who gave you birth rejoice." If you don't transform your pain you will transmit your pain. Richard Rohr

Pain and feeling lost,
but smiling for my children.

This is the day that I went to my mother-in-law and my family to tell them that my husband had left the children and I. I had not heard from him in two months. It was hard to admit and I was scared because I didn't know how we were going to make it. In 1970, I went from an income of $30,000.00 to $6,000.00. It took 14 years to get back to a salary of $30,000.00

This is my mother-in-law Dorothy and her husband Albert who loved me, supported me and encourage me and the children to hold on until our change came.

My husband's family surrounded me with love and support. Each one found a way to help me without offending me.

My son Damon and his wife Antoinette have been counseling and mentoring youth for 24 years. He is now pastoring and they are counseling together.

"Also I heard the voice of the Lord saying who shall I send and who will go for us?" Then said I, "Here am I send me." Isaiah 6:8.

Give Wise Council

Pour your love, faith, time, talent and your money into your grandchildren and all the children in your village. Share your testimony with your children, let them know what you have been through and what God has done for you.

The picture below is my granddaughter, Ebony. Her grandmother Carther is teaching her proper table manners. Ebony has always listened to her parents and grandparents.

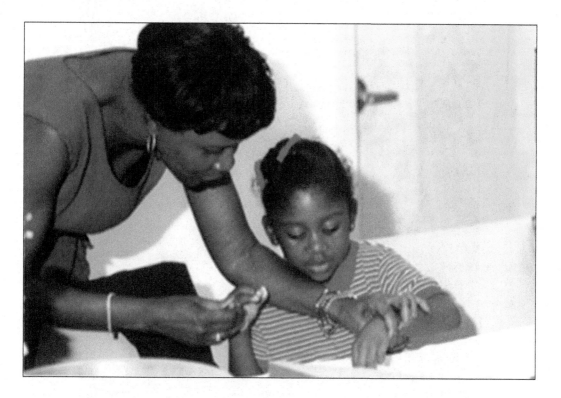

Ebony is 20 years old and in her senior year of college, doing well.

Look at Me

This is what each child should be able to say to their younger siblings and friends.

Below my granddaughter Destiny is congratulating her big sister Ebony graduating from high school. Destiny bought two lockets and put a picture of her sister and herself in each locket. She said she wanted them to wear the lockets until her sister comes home from college.

Destiny loves and respects her big sister, and Ebony knows her sister is watching her.

Celebrating The Children In Our Village

This is my granddaughter Kendra in the picture below, she is graduating from middle school. She knew her family and friends were proud of her and had great expectations for her future. She graduated from Temple University in 2011 with a degree in communications, concentrating in journalism and broadcasting.

Parents with Visions

Ben's mother named him Benjamin Franklin because she had great visions for his life.

This is my brother Ben talking to his grandson. Ben was a great pharmacist, but he may be telling his grandson to become a pilot because Ben enjoyed flying.

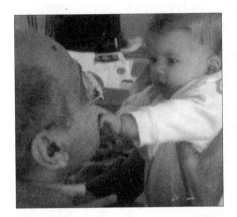

This picture below is Ben and his friend who is a pilot and owns his own plane. Ben enjoyed flying with his friend.

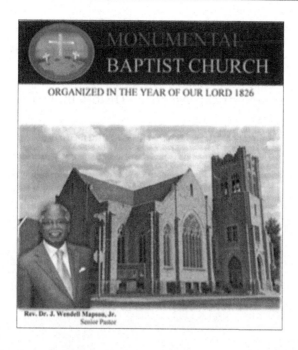

Monumental started with 6 members in 1826, in the home of Rev. George Black. I was told that the church served as an Underground Railroad during slavery in the 1800's.

"It takes a village to raise a child, and it takes a church to raise a village."

Monumental Baptist Church has been serving God and making a difference in our community for 190 years. It moved to this edifice in 1967.

This is a picture of Rev. M.M. Peace. My pastor at Monumental Baptist Church for more than 50 years. He is talking to my mother Lenora Drummond.

I've learned that blessings come through the chain of authority.

Mrs. Irene Morgan is 90 years old. She joined Monumental Baptist Church in 1936.

She has been singing in the choir and mentoring young women in the church and her community for approximately 75 years.

Our church celebrates African-American History in the month of February and we all wear African garb.

Her two daughters Trudy and Georgette sing her praise.

Two of My Heroes

Cousin Josephine Brewton (left, deceased) and Mrs. Bertha McMurray (right), who continues to mentor me. They continued to mentor me after my mother died when I was fifty years old. I learned that I hadn't outgrown the need for mentors and role models because they have already been down a road that I still have to travel.

Children need real live heroes in their lives.

Monumental Baptist Church in 1989 my granddaughter Kendra was dedicated by Rev. Dr. Wendell Mapson, Jr.

It's a Family Affair

My pastor, Rev. Dr. Wendell Mapson, Jr. of now twenty-eight years. Cousin Sylvia Nixon

Kendra held by her mother Kenya, Cousin's Allen, Sandra, and me, I'm the third generation in Monumental.

We should continue to dedicate our babies to Christ, as we live by our faith in front of them. It provides a hedge of protection around our children.

Strongholds in The Ghetto

Churches are the main stronghold in the black community.
Monumental Baptist Church sits in the so called "ghetto" in West Philadelphia.
But we give our children hope, faith, values, and standards to live by.
We create activities to help our children learn and express themselves through singing, dancing, drama, poster contest and the speaker's contest. The choir and ushering teach discipline.

Michelle Clayton Hardy

Center Stage Above, playing Dorothy in the Wizard of Oz

Leadership Training

The young people in Monumental Baptist are trained to be Trustees, Deacons, and Deaconesses. My church started a college scholarship fund in the 1970s and many of our young people have returned to Monumental as leaders. Some are leaders in their church and community in the cities where they have relocated.

Professionally, they are now doctors, nurses, lawyers, engineers, movie produces, service men and women in the military, CEO's, teachers, college professors, accountants, equal employment specialist, airline pilots and flight attendants, ministers and pastors, actors, professional basketball players, music producers, and the graphic design artist are moving our churches communication into the 21st Century.

Now our young people are being trained as audio technicians and in radio broadcasting and developing our church website and newsletters. They are also planting gardens and learning about healthy lifestyles.

The second picture below is Clifton Braxton and Michael Weston participating in our Black History program in the 1990s. Clifton is a lawyer and Michael is making a career in the service.

My mentor.

This is Aunt Hazel. The only survivor left from the house of the war brides.
She instilled the importance of knowing my family history and our history as black people. She has traveled extensively and she sparked my interest in traveling and studying other cultures.

It is because of mentors like Aunt Hazel that I was eager to join the local Alliance of Black Social Workers and the National Association of Black Social Workers. We convene in different states and abroad to study and understand the culture, traditions, and legislation across the diaspora that effect black people. We wear African Garb for the entire week because our African Heritage is what we all have in common.

National Association of Black Social Workers Conference.

Afrocentric Dignity and Pride

Left to Right: Dr. Miriam Monges (deceased), Dr. Thad Mathis, and Sister Orneice Leslie (deceased)

Left: Dr. Gloria Baptiste and Dr. Morris Jeff(deceased), both past presidents of NABSW.

The National Alliance of Black Social Workers celebrate our heritage through history, art, music, dress and dance at our conferences.

Left Julie, Philadelphia Conference Chair   Black Indians of New Orleans

Lois, President, Philadelphia Alliance and me.

Artistic Coat and Heads of Black Women on pocket books

More Black Indians in New Orleans

My friend Veronica Rucker, then a student at Rutgers University of Camden, invited me on this trip. She is standing in front of a cabin in the Etosha Park Safari Lodge in Namibia, South Africa watching the animals graze. The air conditioned cabins were beautiful inside.

I went on Safari in Winhoek and climbed sand dunes in the Cape of Good Hope.

The Dobra resettlement camp, near Windhoek, first stop for Namibians returning from Angola and Zambia.

We saw black people migrating from the Bush to be near the city.

The Government built them cement huts.

Similar to the grass huts they lived in the bush.

Minds Sharpens Minds

I met Kevin when I went to South Africa in 1996. He invited my friend Vonnie and I to his house for dinner and his parents came and gave us their history in South Africa.

Kevin came to visit me in my home in 1998. This is a picture of him and my friend Yvonne Mann.

Kevin was appointed the President of the first trade school open to blacks around 1995. He and Yvonne are exchanging information on the struggle of emancipation after slavery and apartheid ends.

He was not aware of our history through slavery, reconstruction, Jim Crow, segregation and the civil rights era of the 50's and 60's and continuing today.

Coming to America

Kevin and his family, his wife Lisa, daughter Kim and son little Kevin. They had never seen snow. They enjoyed every moment of the snow, driving from Washington to N.Y. to Phila., then to Florida to Disney World, experiencing all 4 seasons in one trip.

Kevin and his son enjoyed the car show in Philadelphia, and the Franklin Institute.

Travel, enjoy and learn from other cultures from other parts of the world.

This is Kevin and Lisa's daughter Kim on the left and my granddaughter Kendra on the right, they were both twelve years old. They knew and enjoyed the same movies, music, dance and style of clothing. They also looked alike. We were amazed at all of the things they had in common.

Kenya is reading a tribute to me at my surprise 59th birthday party. The theme was "Who can find a virtuous woman". In the above picture she is reading Proverbs 31. In the picture below she had the family chauffeured by the Jeffrey Smith Pure Glass limousine service. My friend Nellie's son.

My daughter and I, Minister Kenya Halliday.

A righteous man will fall seven times, but he will rise again. An unrighteous man will fall one time and descend into depression and destitution.

Proverbs 24:16

Stay In Touch

My granddaughter Kyra lives in Maryland, but she stays in touch with me in Philadelphia.

She is now eighteen years old, but she enjoys calling to check on her grand-mother, and keeping me up to date on her activities and accomplishments.

I did not die because I had more work to do.
These are my great- grandbabies:
Kayliana on the left, 7
Kapri on the right, 5

My daughter Kenya and granddaughter Kendra parasailing in the Bahamas on Kendra's 16th birthday.

Enjoy Life

Be able to laugh at yourself, laughter is the best medicine for all that ails you.

Thank you Mommy!!!

I am holding my mother's hand as she is dying.

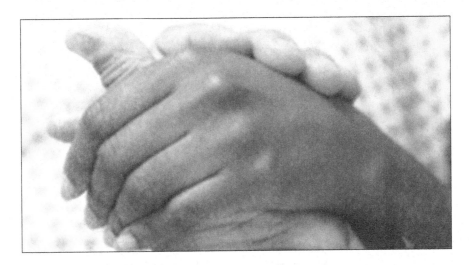

When I am making important decisions I will always hear your voice asking "And what will you give in exchange for your soul." Matthew 16:26

I thank my readers and I hope it encourages you to write your story. Our children should have our legacy.

Thanks

CPSIA information can be obtained
at www.ICGtesting.com
Printed in the USA
BVOW10s1939270516

449863BV00002B/2/P